1

9/11 and the New York City economy: A borough-by-borough analysis

The effect of the terrorist attacks of September 11, 2001,
on the New York City economy was far reaching and extended
to every borough of the city; hardest hit was New York's "export"
sector—the most internationally oriented part of that economy

Michael L. Dolfman
and
Solidelle F. Wasser

The political, security, and social implications of the terrorist attack of September 11, 2001, have been well documented. In New York City, the events of that day resulted in the deaths of 2,699 workers from a wide range of occupational backgrounds. Of the 2,198 non-rescue workers killed in the World Trade Center, 78 percent were employed in finance, insurance, and real estate. Firefighters accounted for 81 percent of the 412 fatally injured rescue workers; 15 percent were police officers or detectives. Thirty-six percent of the 89 individuals killed on the airplanes that crashed into the towers were traveling on services-related business.[1]

The terrorist attack also had a profound impact on the city's economy, its labor market dynamics, and individual businesses. Just what the immediate and long-term economic effects of the attack were and will be on New York City has been the subject of some debate. This article joins that discussion in its analysis of employment and wage data, on a borough-by-borough basis.

The article focuses on the most salient feature of the current city economy: the bifurcation of its industry into "export" and "local" economic sectors.[2] Examining the effect of 9/11 on each of the boroughs makes it possible to isolate the "export" sector, on the one hand, which identifies New York City as a prime center of the global economy, and the "local" sector, on the other, which has its own distinct importance and relation to the city's industry.

In what follows, trends in employment and wage patterns based on the Bureau of Labor Statistics (BLS) Quarterly Census of Employment and Wages (QCEW) program are compared, on a borough-by-borough basis, before and after the attack to measure the extent of the losses. The relation of these losses to the entire New York economy completes the analysis.

Understanding the city's economy

In order to comprehend fully the economic impact of the 9/11 attack on New York, it is important to place the recent labor market economy of the city in the context of the developmental forces that began to emerge 30 years earlier. Among the most noteworthy of these forces was the international movement toward a global economy.

Thirty years ago, globalization, as we currently understand it, was beginning to emerge. Although close to bankruptcy in the 1970s, New York was poised to take advantage of these new perspectives. Specifically, the emergence of, and increase in, the complexity of international transactions raised the scale of economic growth and stirred the need for multinational headquarters functions. In addition, the demand that firms across all industry sectors provide specialized services stimulated the need for financial, marketing, accounting, legal, telecommunication, insurance, computer, and management consulting services.[3]

Michael L. Dolfman is Regional Commissioner for Economic Analysis and Information, New York Regional Office, Bureau of Labor Statistics, New York, New York; Solidelle F. Wasser is a senior economist in the same office. E-mail: Dolfman. Michael@bls.gov

New York City industry has long been international, but its role is becoming increasingly evident as the world's economy places a premium on the free movement of knowledge, ideas, capital, labor, and technology, as opposed to just the exchange and production of commodities. The new North American Industrial Classification System (NAICS) focuses on those factors which better define the elements of the global economy; accordingly, the NAICS figures prominently in the analysis that follows.

Today, in analyzing the economic effects of globalization, attention is usually directed at increases in the mobility of capital, particularly across international borders, and at the power of emerging information technologies. New York, by virtue of its dual international and national orientation, was a prime U.S. beneficiary of these global forces. The international trade and global financial investment activities of the city stimulated further its leadership position in marketing and advertising, finance and banking, broadcasting, information technology, publishing, real estate, and a host of other arenas. In addition, recent literature on global power centers (often called "global cities") notes that an increase in local public administration functions fills the gap created by weakening national regulation.[4] Government employment figures in New York reflect this increasing trend.[5]

By the beginning of the 21st century, New York City's economy was mature and sophisticated. The "export" sector—finance and insurance; professional, scientific, and technical occupations; information; arts, entertainment, and recreation; the management of companies; real estate; and what was left of manufacturing—was focused nationally and internationally, while the "local" market sector—administrative and support, and waste; construction; wholesale and retail trade; transportation and warehousing; utilities; educational services; health care and social assistance; and accommodation and food services—had a regional orientation. Both economies made important contributions to the city and the welfare of its citizens, but it was the "export" sector that gave New York its special place among international cities—its appeal, its reputation, its glamour, and its wealth.

The tragic events of 9/11 had a significant impact on the economy and labor market of New York City, and its repercussions were felt throughout the country. The effects of the attack, along with a weakening national and global economy, helped to create an extremely volatile economic environment in the city.

The expansion that characterized the city's economy during the decade of the 1990s started to lose momentum during January 2001. The downturn, with its subsequent loss of jobs, began in May 2001 and continued beyond December 2002.

The discussion that follows indicates that the effect of 9/11 is clear, unambiguous, and independent of the national recession. In particular, the economic downturn in the city was sharper than could have been anticipated from just the general economic contraction.

Within the city, the attack resulted in about 430,000 lost job months and a loss in wages of $2.8 billion.[6] These lost job months were equivalent to approximately 143,000 jobs, each month, for 3 months. The effect of 9/11 was centered on the city's "export" economy, which represented 68.0 percent of all lost job months and 86.0 percent of all lost wages.

Manhattan

In 2000, Manhattan, like the city and the Nation, was riding a wave of economic expansion that began in the 1990s. However, the relationship between jobs and wages in the borough was different from that experienced in the Nation as a whole. For the country as a whole, wages had remained relatively flat between 1978 and 2000, while employment growth was marked and consistent. For Manhattan, the converse was true: employment growth had remained essentially level, while wages increased substantially. Chart 1 illustrates these distinctions, by comparing changes in average employment with changes in real wages for the United States and for Manhattan.[7]

Manhattan was known for its high-paying jobs, and its rising wages proved to be a magnet. Manhattan became unique in the number of jobs it supported. Among the core counties of all the Consolidated Metropolitan Statistical Areas (CMSA's) in the Nation, Manhattan was the only one in which the number of people who worked there was greater than the local resident population.

In 2000, wage and salary employment in Manhattan approached 2.4 million workers. (See table 1.) Payroll jobs in the borough amounted to two-thirds of all jobs in New York City and one-sixth of the jobs in the 31-county CMSA. One-and-one-half million people resided in the borough, of whom the 2000 census reported that some 600,000 worked in Manhattan. The local resident population was thus only a fraction of a larger economic enterprise. The following tabulation gives the location of residence of the Manhattan workforce in 2000:[8]

Residence	Number	Percent
Manhattan	631,132	26.5
Other New York City counties	900,336	37.8
Outside of city	850,698	35.7

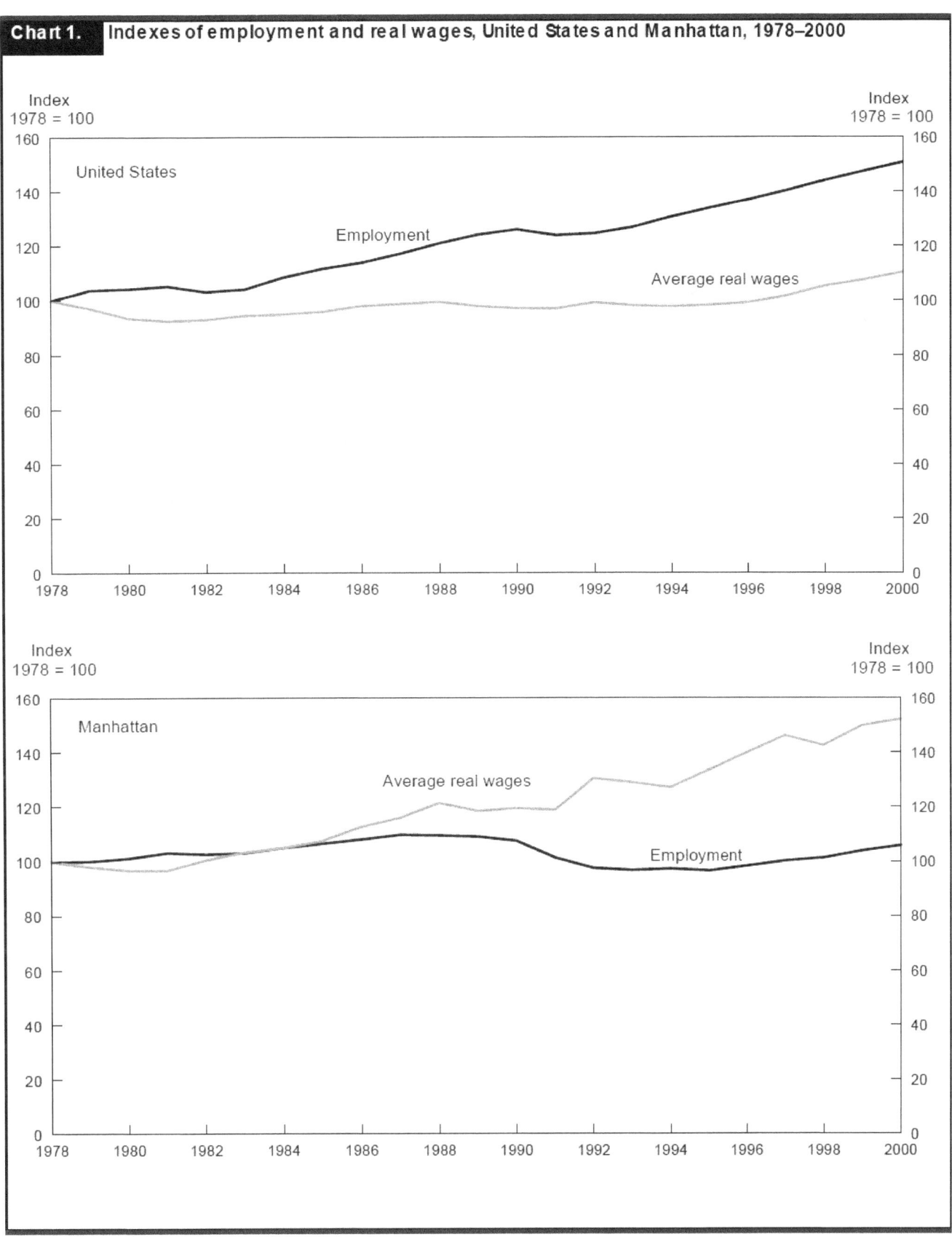

Chart 1. Indexes of employment and real wages, United States and Manhattan, 1978–2000

Table 1.	Trends in jobs, population, and wages, Manhattan, 2000 and 2002		
Category	Number or amount		
	2000	2002	
Total jobs	2,382,166	2,249,140	
Total population	1,537,195	1,546,856	
Total wages	$172,879,553,256	$161,029,255,538	
Average wage	$72,572	$71,596	

Sources: Job and wage data—BLS QCEW program; population data—U.S. Census Bureau website http://eire.census.gov/popest/data/counties/CO-EST2003-01php (visited April 2003).

A look at employment distribution in Manhattan shows that more than 40 percent of all jobs there in 2000 were in the "export" sector—25.7 percent were in finance and insurance and the professional, scientific, and technical NAICS sectors alone (see table 2)—giving support to the importance of the "export" sector to the overall Manhattan economy. In total, "export" jobs represented 66.4 percent of all borough wages, with the finance and professional services sectors alone accounting for almost half the total.

In the finance and insurance sector, yearly wages averaged $186,097 in 2000, with wages in finance alone averaging $206,758.[9] Average wages in the professional, scientific, and technical sector were $84,244. Within this sector, jobs in management and technical consulting services averaged $110,073, jobs in advertising and related services $92,194, jobs in computer systems design and related services $89,015, and jobs in legal services $87,402. Although employment in the sector designated "management of companies" represented only 2.0 percent of all jobs, average wages were high ($158,461), and the sector accounted for 4.3 percent of all wages. (See table 2.)

By 2002, Manhattan's economy was in decline. Although the borough's population had increased slightly from the 2000 figure, total jobs declined 5.6 percent (133,026), total wages declined 6.9 percent, and the average wage declined 1.3 percent. (See table 1.) During the same period, the All Items Consumer Price Index (CPI) for the New York area increased 5.2 percent, making the decline in real wages about 6.5 percent. The effects of this economic downturn were not shared equally across all sectors.

Between 2000 and 2002, the Manhattan economy lost 133,026 jobs and $11,850,297,717 in wages, with 82.7 percent of the job declines and 111.0 percent of the lost wages associated with the "export" economy. (Increases in wages in "local"-economy jobs magnified the wage loss effect registered by "export"-economy jobs.) Losses in the "export" sector clearly damaged and weakened Manhattan's economic linkages with the Nation and the international community, but, more importantly, altered the borough's unique character. In fact, more than 1 out of every 4 Manhattan jobs lost came from the finance and insurance sector alone, with another quarter lost from professional, scientific, and technical services.

The "export" industries

Finance and insurance. In 2002, 293,635 Manhattan jobs were in the finance and insurance sector. (See table 2.) In fact, 9 out of 10 jobs in the sector in New York City were located in Manhattan. The finance and insurance sector thus still accounted for 13.1 percent of all Manhattan jobs, although now only slightly more than 32.2 percent of Manhattan wages. Since 2000, 35,209 jobs had been lost in the sector, or 10.7 percent of its employment base. Average wages declined 5.0 percent (10.2 percent, adjusted for increases in the CPI), to $176,837.

In finance alone, total jobs declined 11.6 percent, and the average nominal wage fell 5.9 percent, to $194,563. However, it appears that the job reductions recorded within the sector—as measured by wages—may not have been proportional across employment categories.[10] Table 3 gives a breakdown of the average monthly employment and the average wage in various employment categories within the finance sector.

Professional, technical, and scientific occupations. In New York City in 2002, 89.8 percent of all jobs in the professional, technical, and scientific sector were located in Manhattan. The sector accounted for 11.1 percent of all Manhattan jobs and 13.6 percent of all Manhattan wages. From 2000 to 2002, the sector lost 34,029 jobs (1 out of every 4 Manhattan jobs lost), or 12.0 percent of its job base. However, average wages rose 4.2 percent, to $87,782. Table 3 presents the average monthly employment and the average wage in various employment categories in the professional, technical, and scientific services sector.

For many years, the finance industry, and Wall Street in particular, has been Manhattan's "hometown" industry and driving economic force. Manhattan employment in the SIC-classified security and commodity brokers portion of this industry had represented about 25 percent of the industry's nationwide employment and about 40 percent of its nationwide payroll. Due to the size of its profits, bonuses, and employment opportunities, analysts have suggested that the security and commodity brokers industry has been the single most determinative factor causing short-term volatility and cyclical change in the Manhattan economy.[11]

Wall Street is a voracious user of legal, accounting, computer, management consulting, printing, and other professional and technical services. On the surface, it would appear that, as Wall Street profits, wages, and jobs declined, the effect would be felt across many of the categories making up the professional, scientific, and technical sector. However, 73.5 percent of the jobs lost in the sector were from just two categories: computer systems design and related services (12,998 jobs) and advertising and related services (12,019 jobs.)

Information. The information sector is a key component of the Manhattan job scene. Between 2000 and 2002, the sector lost 23,351 jobs, or 14.4 percent of its job base. These jobs

Table 2. Employment and wages in selected sectors, Manhattan, 2000 and 2002

Sector	Average monthly employment	Percent of Manhattan employment	Total wages	Percent of total Manhattan wages	Average wage
2000					
Manhattan[1]	2,382,166	100.00	$172,879,553,256	100.00	$72,572
Finance and insurance	328,844	13.80	61,196,930,733	35.40	186,097
Professional, scientific, and technical	284,138	11.93	23,936,793,191	13.85	84,244
Information	162,336	6.82	12,942,762,903	7.49	79,728
Arts, entertainment, and recreation	43,689	1.83	2,238,973,870	1.30	51,248
Management of companies	46,728	1.96	7,404,551,085	4.28	158,461
Real estate, and rental and leasing	75,492	3.17	3,990,265,709	2.31	52,857
Manufacturing	70,022	2.94	3,107,663,164	1.80	44,381
Administrative and support, and waste	155,661	6.53	5,940,016,975	3.44	38,160
Construction	35,489	1.49	2,282,921,413	1.32	64,328
Wholesale trade	90,765	3.81	6,514,702,637	3.77	71,775
Retail trade	133,362	5.80	4,611,290,148	2.67	34,577
Transportation and warehousing	27,805	1.17	1,020,559,006	.59	36,704
Educational services	64,941	2.73	2,736,363,917	1.58	42,136
Health care and social assistance	180,052	7.56	7,299,087,850	4.22	40,539
Accommodation and food services	137,184	5.76	3,665,478,436	2.12	26,719
Other services	82,754	3.47	2,859,744,309	1.65	34,557
Government	453,841	19.05	20,509,510,707	11.86	45,191
Unclassified	3,437	.14	135,512,831	.08	39,428
2002					
Manhattan[1]	2,249,140	100.00	161,029,255,538	100.00	71,596
Finance and insurance	293,635	13.06	51,925,575,579	32.25	176,837
Professional, scientific, and technical	250,109	11.12	21,955,051,846	13.63	87,782
Information	138,985	6.18	11,622,421,137	7.22	83,624
Arts, entertainment, and recreation	43,437	1.93	2,268,773,282	1.41	52,231
Management of companies	50,354	2.24	7,091,329,910	4.40	140,830
Real estate, and rental and leasing	71,891	3.20	3,983,975,512	2.47	55,417
Manufacturing	52,823	2.35	2,776,784,793	1.72	52,568
Administrative and support, and waste	134,026	5.96	5,308,308,206	3.30	39,607
Construction	31,974	1.42	2,202,635,368	1.37	68,888
Wholesale trade	82,566	3.67	6,287,160,465	3.90	76,147
Retail trade	123,477	5.49	4,534,139,745	2.82	36,721
Transportation and warehousing	25,678	1.14	1,028,589,129	.64	40,057
Educational services	72,799	3.24	3,129,007,254	1.94	42,981
Health care and social assistance	192,262	8.55	8,118,447,888	5.04	42,226
Accommodation and food services	132,797	5.90	3,658,016,266	2.27	27,546
Other services	81,393	3.62	3,190,752,753	1.98	39,202
Government	457,926	20.36	21,062,145,527	13.08	45,995
Unclassified	7,267	.32	384,699,699	.24	52,938

[1] Detailed entries do not necessarily sum to totals. (See appendix.)   Source: BLS QCEW program.

represented 17.6 percent of all Manhattan jobs lost. During the same period, despite the significant job loss, average wages increased 4.9 percent, to $83,624. Four components of the sector—newspaper, periodical, book, and directory publishers; motion picture and video industries; radio and television broadcasting; and wired telecommunication carriers— constitute 75.5 percent of the sector's employment base. All components experienced job losses, with concomitant increases in average wages. Table 3 shows the average monthly employment and the average wage in selected employment categories within the information sector.

Arts, entertainment, and recreation. Although containing less than 2 percent of Manhattan's jobs, the arts, entertainment, and recreation sector has always been another high-profile sector of the Manhattan economy. Looking at the sector as a whole and using 2000 as the base, one finds that jobs remained constant, while average wages rose 1.9 percent, to $52,231. For selected categories within the sector, the relationship between jobs and average wages demonstrated greater variation. Table 3 gives a breakdown of the average monthly employment and the average wage in selected employment categories within the arts, entertainment, and recreation sector.

Table 3.	Employment and wages in selected "export" sectors, Manhattan, 2002		
Sector	Average monthly employment	Average wage
Finance		
Depository credit intermediation	42,417	$123,069
Nondepository credit intermedia ion ...	24,055	123,906
Activities related to credit intermediation	4,811	86,136
Securities and commodity contracts brokerage	120,853	244,926
Securities and commodity exchanges	3,406	136,290
O her financial investment activities	39,737	184,395
Professional, scientific, and technical		
Legal services	73,702	94,036
Accounting, tax preparation, bookkeeping, and payroll services ...	31,092	80,741
Architectural, engineering, and related services	19,848	72,377
Specialized design services	9,008	65,509
Computer systems design and related services	29,318	94,785
Management, scientific, and technical consulting services	22,295	109,444
Scientific research and development services	12,099	49,360
Advertising and related services	44,345	93,659
Other professional, scientific, and technical services	8,876	61,848
Information		
Newspaper, periodical, book, and directory publishers	49,651	85,274
Software publishers	1,569	97,929
Motion picture and video industries ...	27,289	72,847
Sound-recording industries	3,823	122,897
Radio and television broadcasting	17,682	87,651
Cable and other subscription programming	5,700	107,445
Wired telecommunications carriers ...	15,129	82,532
Data-processing, hosting, and related services	4,226	86,872
Arts, entertainment, and recreation		
Performing arts companies	13,086	45,648
Promoters of performing arts, sports, and similar events	8,052	66,133
Agents and managers for artists, athletes, entertainers, and other public figures	2,790	90,665
Independent artists, writers, and performers	2,168	139,014
Museums, historical sites, and other institutions	10,690	39,946
SOURCE: BLS QCEW program.		

Manufacturing. One result of globalization is the continuing movement of manufacturing production. By 2002, jobs in the manufacturing sector represented a scant 2.4 percent of the borough's employment base and had fallen to 52,823, a 24.6-percent decline in just 2 years. By contrast, during the same time frame, average wages *rose* 18.4 percent, to $52,568, indicating that there were jobs (for example, fashion designers) so highly skilled and technical that they could not be exported easily.

Two categories dominated what was left of manufacturing in Manhattan in 2002. The garment industry—specifically, cut and sew apparel manufacturing—accounted for 40.6 percent of all jobs within the sector, while printing and related support activities constituted 15.9 percent of the jobs. With 2000 as the base, jobs in apparel manufacturing decreased by 9,626, or 31.0 percent, while average wages increased by $10,396, or 29.0 percent, by 2002. In the printing category, jobs decreased by 1,734, or 17.1 percent, possibly an impact of the Wall Street decline. Average wages, however, remained constant at slightly under $58,000.

The "local" market sectors

Administrative and support, and waste. In 2002, the administrative and support, and waste sector accounted for 6.0 percent of Manhattan's jobs. However, the sector lost 21,635 jobs between 2000 and 2002, 13.9 percent of its job base. Most of the decline was in two categories: employment services, which lost 16,394 jobs (22.9 percent of its job base), and business support services, which lost 2,695 jobs (19.4 percent of its base). The employment services industry includes temporary-help services, a job category that is cyclically related to changes in the business climate. In contrast, investigative and security services recorded an 8.3-percent increase in jobs (1,868) and a 10.7-percent increase in average wages ($23,396) as security concerns intensified in the post-9/11 period. During the 2000–02 period, average wages in the administrative and support, and waste sector increased 3.8 percent, to $39,607.

Retail trade and wholesale trade. In 2002 Manhattan, 5.5 percent of all jobs were in the retail trade sector. From 2000 to 2002, the sector lost 9,885 jobs, or 7.4 percent of its job base. However, during the same period, as appears to be the pattern, average wages rose 6.1 percent, to $36,721.

Within the retail trade sector, four categories—clothing stores, grocery stores, health and personal care establishments, and department stores—provided more than 50 percent of the jobs. Table 4 gives the average monthly employment and the average wage in various employment categories in the retail trade sector.

Wholesale trade provided 3.7 percent (82,566) of all Manhattan jobs in 2002. The sector lost 9.0 percent of its 2000 job base in the 2-year period. During the same time frame, average salaries increased 6.0 percent, from $71,775 to $76,147. In the construction sector and the transportation and warehousing

Table 4.	Employment and wages in selected "local" sectors, Manhattan, 2002		
Sector	Average monthly employment	Average wage
Retail trade		
Electronics and appliance stores	6,615	$50,325
Grocery stores	13,324	21,411
Health and personal care stores	12,895	39,212
Clothing stores	28,532	35,373
Jewelry, luggage, and leather goods stores..	6,481	52,808
Sporting goods and musical instrument stores..	3,629	31,273
Book, periodical, and music stores	4,525	23,771
Office supplies, stationery, and gift stores..	4,022	29,282
Accommodation and food services		
Traveler accommodation	33,102	41,784
Full-service restaurants	64,457	24,901
Limited-service eating places	21,468	15,434
Special food services	8,911	24,501
Drinking places (alcoholic beverages)..	4,625	23,889

SOURCE: BLS QCEW program.

Educational services and health care and social assistance. The trend of job declines and wage increases did not extend to all major sectors. In educational services and in health care and social assistance, both the average number of jobs and average annual wages increased between 2000 and 2002. In education, jobs rose 12.1 percent, to 72,799, and average wages inched up 2.0 percent, to $42,981. In the health care and social assistance sector, which accounted for 8.5 percent of all 2002 Manhattan jobs, jobs increased 6.8 percent, to 12,210, and average wages rose 4.2 percent, to $42,226.

Accommodation and food services. During 2002, the accommodation and food services sector constituted 5.9 percent of all Manhattan jobs, providing services to New York City residents while catering to the tourist industry. The 2-year loss of 4,387 jobs was not shared equally by all categories within the sector; the unbalanced situation pointed up the fact that New Yorkers appear to have been patronizing, to a greater extent, lower cost limited-service eating places, which saw an employment increase of 2.8 percent. Table 4 lists the average monthly employment and the average wage in selected employment categories within the accommodation and food services sector. Table 5 sums up the average monthly employment, total wages, and average wage for all the components of Manhattan's "export" and "local" economies.

sector, which together accounted for 2 percent of all 2002 Manhattan jobs, the trend was the same: a decrease in jobs and an increase in average wages.

Table 5.	Employment and wages in the "export" and "local" sectors, Manhattan, 2000		
Sector	Average monthly employment	Total wages	Average wage
"Export" sector:[1]			
Total	901,349	$101,631,381,694	$112,755
Finance and insurance	293,635	51,925,575,579	176,837
Professional, scientific, and technical	250,109	21,955,051,846	87,782
Information	138,985	11,622,421,137	83,624
Arts, entertainment, and recreation	43,437	2,268,773,282	52,231
Management of companies	50,354	7,091,329,910	140,830
Real estate, and rental and leasing	71,891	3,983,975,512	55,417
Manufacturing	52,823	2,776,784,793	52,568
"Local" sector:[1]			
Total	1,802,583	203,255,293,753	112,758
Administrative and support, and waste	134,026	5,308,308,206	39,607
Construction	31,974	2,202,635,368	68,888
Wholesale trade	82,566	6,287,160,465	76,147
Retail trade	123,477	4,534,139,745	36,721
Transportation and warehousing	25,678	1,028,589,129	40,057
Educational services	72,799	3,129,007,254	42,981
Health care and social assistance	192,262	8,118,447,888	42,226
Accommodation and food services	132,797	3,658,016,266	27,546
Other services	81,393	3,190,752,753	39,202
Government	457,926	21,062,145,527	45,995
Unclassified	7,267	384,699,699	52,938

[1] Detailed entries do not necessarily sum to totals. (See appendix.)   SOURCE: BLS QCEW program.

Issues

By January 2001, 2 months before the nationally recognized March downturn, hiring in Manhattan had begun to decline.[12] Less than 9 months later, the borough was shocked by the terrorist attack. Within 2 weeks of the September 11 attack, the destruction of the World Trade Center and collateral office space led to the movement to New Jersey of 3,319 Manhattan jobs, more than 80 percent of which were in the finance sector. By the end of October, the number had risen to 17,178 jobs. By December 2002, all but 5,204 of those jobs had returned to New York.[13] However, the impact of the terrorist attack went beyond such measures and influenced the course of a recession that was already underway. Clearly, both events influenced the economic downturn characterized by lost jobs and wages. However, in order to gain a clearer picture as to what took place, it is useful to separate the economic effects of the recession from those of the attack.

Methodology

To gain a dynamic picture of employment changes, this section presents a number of charts, each displaying a monthly time series of over-the-year employment changes. Monthly data from January 2000 to December 2002 summarize employment and total pay (exclusive of benefits) of workers covered by State and Federal unemployment insurance. Coverage is broad and is estimated to include 99.7 percent of all wage and salary employees working in the five New York City boroughs over the 3-year period.

The methodology compares employment levels in the current month with those of the same month in the preceding year between January 2001 and December 2002. (The 36 data points are thus reduced to 24 in the charts.) This approach overcomes problems associated with seasonal patterns in employment data that are not seasonally adjusted.

The first point in each chart, January 2001, corresponds to the beginning of the recession in New York. A trend line is inferred from data from January 2001 to September 2001, the first 9 months of the year. (A 9-month period that includes September 2001 is used to construct the trend line, because September employment data, under the QCEW program, would not have included losses stemming from the terrorist attack.)

The charts are examined to see whether, beginning in October 2001, any deviation from the trend line shown took place. If so, this deviation is considered to be related to the effect of 9/11. The economic effects of the deviation are then calculated by geometric methods.

A visual illustration

The trend-line analysis suggests that a distinct alteration in the employment pattern for Manhattan—a change independent of the 2001 recession—commenced after September 11, 2001. (See chart 2.) The duration of this disruption—that is, the influence of 9/11—is seen to have been 4 months, from October 2001 through January 2002. (Note that the Manhattan economy was still losing jobs as of December 2002.)

In particular, the trend-line analysis indicates that the events of September 11 exacerbated the already deteriorating Manhattan economy. On the basis of the trend line for the remainder of 20001, the pace of job loss accelerated and remained gereater than expected. By the end of the year, the acceleration in job loss had moderated. Then, during 2002, although the rate of job loss decelerated, Manhattan was still losing jobs in December.

The analysis further suggests that the attack caused a sharper drop in jobs than would have been expected on the basis of the existing downtrend. It is this difference between the actual job loss experienced over the period from October 2001 to February 2002 and the loss predicted by the trend line that is used to gauge the effect of the events of September 11 on the New York labor market.

Dividing the Manhattan economy into the "export" sector and the "local" sector demonstrates the relation discussed previously. The curve for the "export" sector shows the same 4-month 9/11 effect for Manhattan as a whole, while that for the "local" sector indicates that the effect of 9/11 lasted for 3 months and that the entire sector actually began to add jobs by the end of 2002. (See chart 3.)

The terrorist attack of 9/11 cost the Manhattan economy 238,725 lost job months (the equivalent of 59,681 jobs each month for 4 months) and $2,189,929,660 in lost wages. (See table 6.) A breakdown of specific key sectors points out the differing effects of 9/11, in terms of lost jobs and lost wages, on the various sectors of the Manhattan economy.

Sectors within the "export" economy, in the aggregate, accounted for 65.1 percent of the lost job months and 88.0 percent of the lost wages, while specific sectors within the "local" economy accounted for 34.9 percent of the lost job months and 12.0 percent of lost wages. (Note, however, that three sectors within the "local" economy experienced gains in employment and subsequent gains in wages that tended to dissipate the overall effects of the economic downturn.) The finance sector was clearly a major force in the decline in the Manhattan economy, accounting for 29.3 percent of all lost job months and 55.1 percent of all lost wages. The curve of over-the-year-changes in employment in the sector, shown in the top panel of chart 4, puts the matter in clearer perspective.

Although growth was slowing down somewhat before the attack, the finance sector did not actually begin to shed jobs until September 2001, 8 months after the beginning of the recession. A steep decline in employment at that time is visible, and it is evident that the decline did not bottom out until August 2002. As of December 2002, jobs were still being lost.

At issue is how much of the loss should be attributed to the effects of 9/11. Clearly, the terrorist attack had a significant impact on the finance sector. However, other variables, such as the decline in the American and international stock markets,

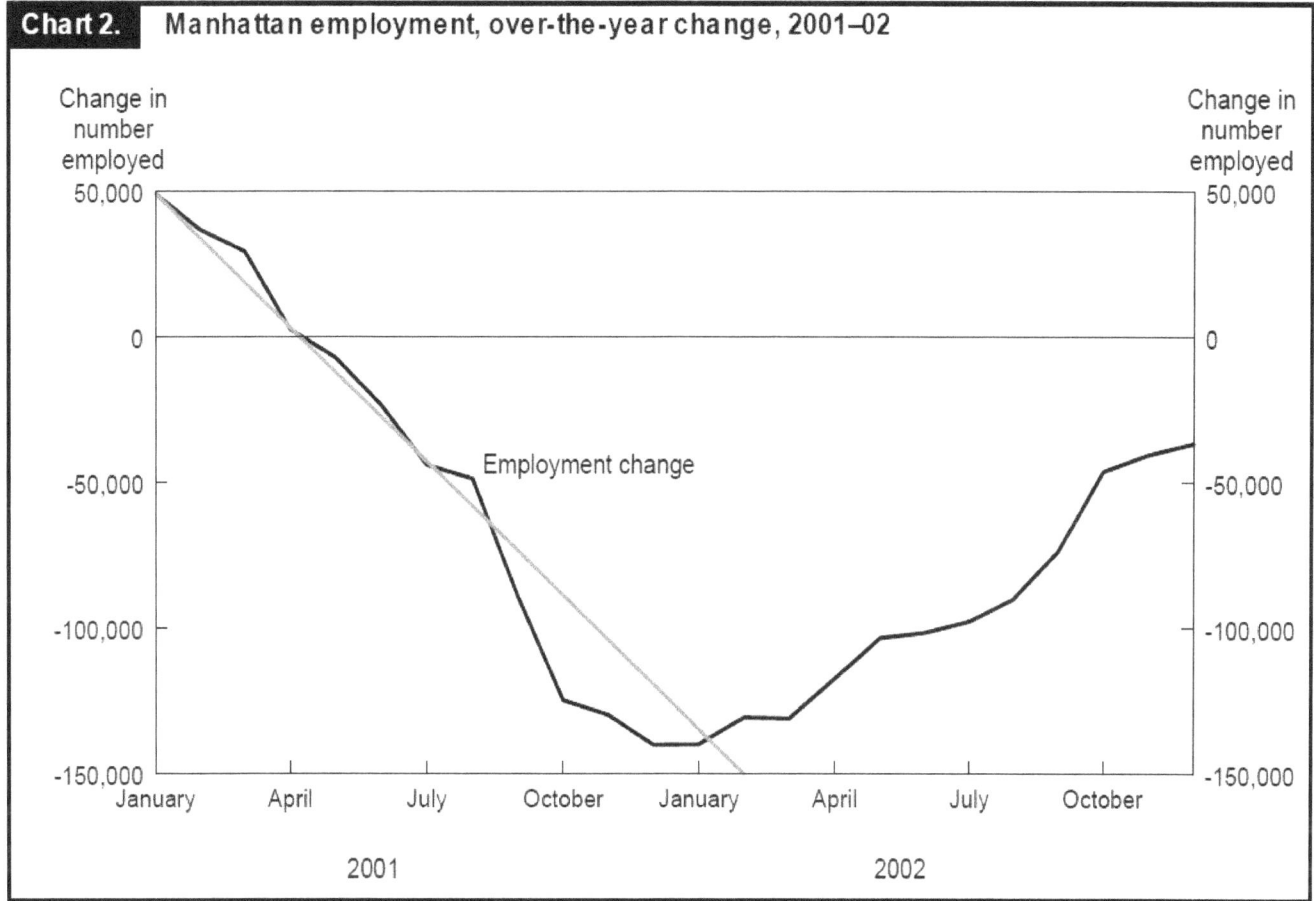

Chart 2. Manhattan employment, over-the-year change, 2001–02

corporate scandals, the war in Afghanistan, the buildup to the war in Iraq, and a drop in overall consumer confidence, also exerted important influences on Manhattan's job losses. In this analysis, it is postulated that the effect of 9/11 on finance was 4 months, the average for the "export" sector.[14] The continued decline after January 2002 is attributed to other factors. Although the finance sector was the dominant sector that was affected by the terrorist attack, other sectors were as well.

Professional, scientific, and technical services. The close relationship between this sector and the finance sector already has been discussed, but the effect of the 9/11 terrorist attack on the professional, scientific, and technical services sector was markedly different from that experienced by the finance sector. Professional, scientific, and technical services began to lose jobs in April 2001, and the sector was already in steep decline by September 2001. In reality, the effect of 9/11 on this sector was marginal. (Recall that the loss of jobs in the sector was due in large measure to the economic collapse of the computer/"dot-com industry" and declines in advertising services and thus was related to the business cycle.) By December, just like the finance

sector, the professional, scientific, and technical sector was still shedding jobs and losing wages. (See chart 4, second panel.)

Accommodation and food services. Although most food service establishments rely heavily on local customers, Manhattan's tourist industry and employment in its critical accommodation and food services sector were severely affected by the 9/11 attack. Job losses had begun in the sector during August 2001 and were pronounced and precipitous. The losses bottomed out in November 2001, but still continued until September 2002, when positive job growth was recorded. (See chart 4, third panel.)

Government. Following the terrorist attack, the Federal Government provided assistance to Manhattan and, indeed, the entire city. Employees from Federal law en-forcement, intelligence, immigration, economic development, and disaster assistance agencies converged on the city, ultimately pumping just under $98 million dollars into the Manhattan economy for expenditures for food, lodging, and other ne-cessities. The bottom panel of chart 4 suggests that Federal work-ers may have been on 3-month assignment blocks.

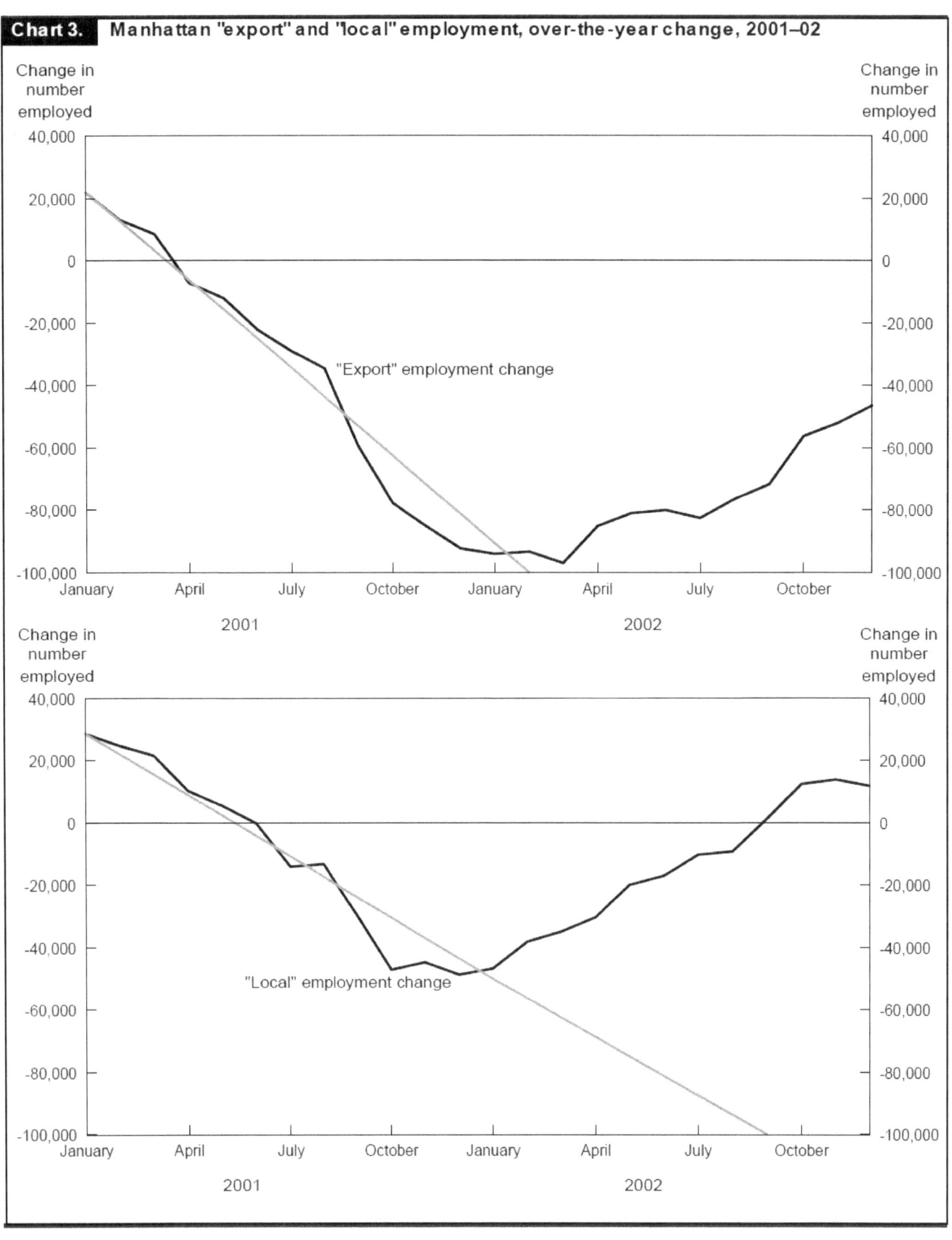

Chart 3. Manhattan "export" and "local" employment, over-the-year change, 2001–02

Table 6.	Effect of 9/11 in job months and lost or gained wages over the 2000–02 period, Manhattan	
Sector	Job months	Wages, lost or gained
Total lost[1]	−238,725	−$2,189,929,660
Finance and insurance	−96,000	−1,514,082,000
Finance	−70,000	−1,206,556,000
Professional, scientific, and technical	−16,000	−116,032,000
Information	−32,000	−223,828,000
Arts, entertainment, and recreation	−5,500	−24,103,500
Management of companies	−2,350	−34,037,100
Real estate, and rental and leasing	−3,450	−15,936,300
Wholesale trade	−11,500	−71,503,500
Retail trade	−8,400	−25,250,400
Transportation and warehousing	−2,175	−6,699,000
Health care and social assistance	−8,850	−30,591,900
Accommodation and food services	−45,500	−102,647,000
Other services	−6,000	−18,306,000
Total gained	32,250	127,045,250
Construction	2,750	15,726,500
Educational services	4,000	13,577,250
Government	25,500	97,741,500

[1] Detailed entries do not necessarily sum to totals. (See appendix.) SOURCE: BLS QCEW program.

The other boroughs

With two-thirds of all New York City jobs located in Manhattan, any study of the city's economy will inevitably be heavily influenced by developments taking place there. Of special interest in this analysis, however, is the economic effect of 9/11 on *each* of the city's boroughs. Accordingly, in what follows, patterns of "export" and "local" employment will be examined to determine (1) to what extent each borough's experience was similar or dissimilar to Manhattan's; (2) how each borough individually relates to New York City as a global center; and (3) what specific effect, if any, the terrorist attack of 9/11 had on each borough's economy.

Queens

In 2000, Queens, like Manhattan, the city, and, indeed, the Nation, was in the midst of an economic boom. The job growth that had begun in the early 1990s caused the number of jobs to reach 480,676, a 23-year high, in 2000. Unlike the situation in Manhattan, the relationship between employment and wages in Queens resembled that of the Nation as a whole. From 1978 to 2000, employment had risen, while real wages had remained relatively constant. (See chart 5.) Indeed, in terms of real wages, the average wage in Queens in 2000 was less than it was in 1978. (For comparison, however, note that real wages in the Nation did not exceed 1978 levels until 1997.)

Queens had benefited from the greater labor mobility of the global economy. More than 46 percent of the borough's population was foreign born. Between 1995 and 2000, about 175,000 people from abroad had settled in Queens. Between 2001 and 2002, the population of the borough was augmented by approximately 40,000 additional foreign arrivals,[15] offsetting a population loss resulting from net negative internal migration. This influx of workers from another wage structure may account in part for the sluggish behavior of wages in Queens: to fully realize one's skills takes time, even when greater opportunities for their realization exist.

Queens' 480,676 jobs (see table 7) represented 13.3 percent of New York City's employment base. With the city's two airports—John F. Kennedy and LaGuardia—located within the borough's boundaries, 55.0 percent of all New York City jobs in the transportation and warehousing sector were found in Queens.

Again unlike the situation in Manhattan, where a large percentage of the borough's workers lived outside of New York City and were attracted to Manhattan by its high wages, the percentage of Queens workers living outside of New York City was only 20.6 percent. Those living and working in Queens constituted 61.7 percent of the borough's workforce, and those living in other New York City counties made up 17.7 percent of Queens' workforce.[16]

An examination of employment distribution in Queens reveals that three sectors—health care and social assistance; transportation and warehousing; and retail trade (all classified as "local" market sectors)—accounted for 44.7 percent of all borough jobs. (See table 8.) The average wage in Queens in 2000, $34,986, was 51.8 percent lower than the average wage in Manhattan.

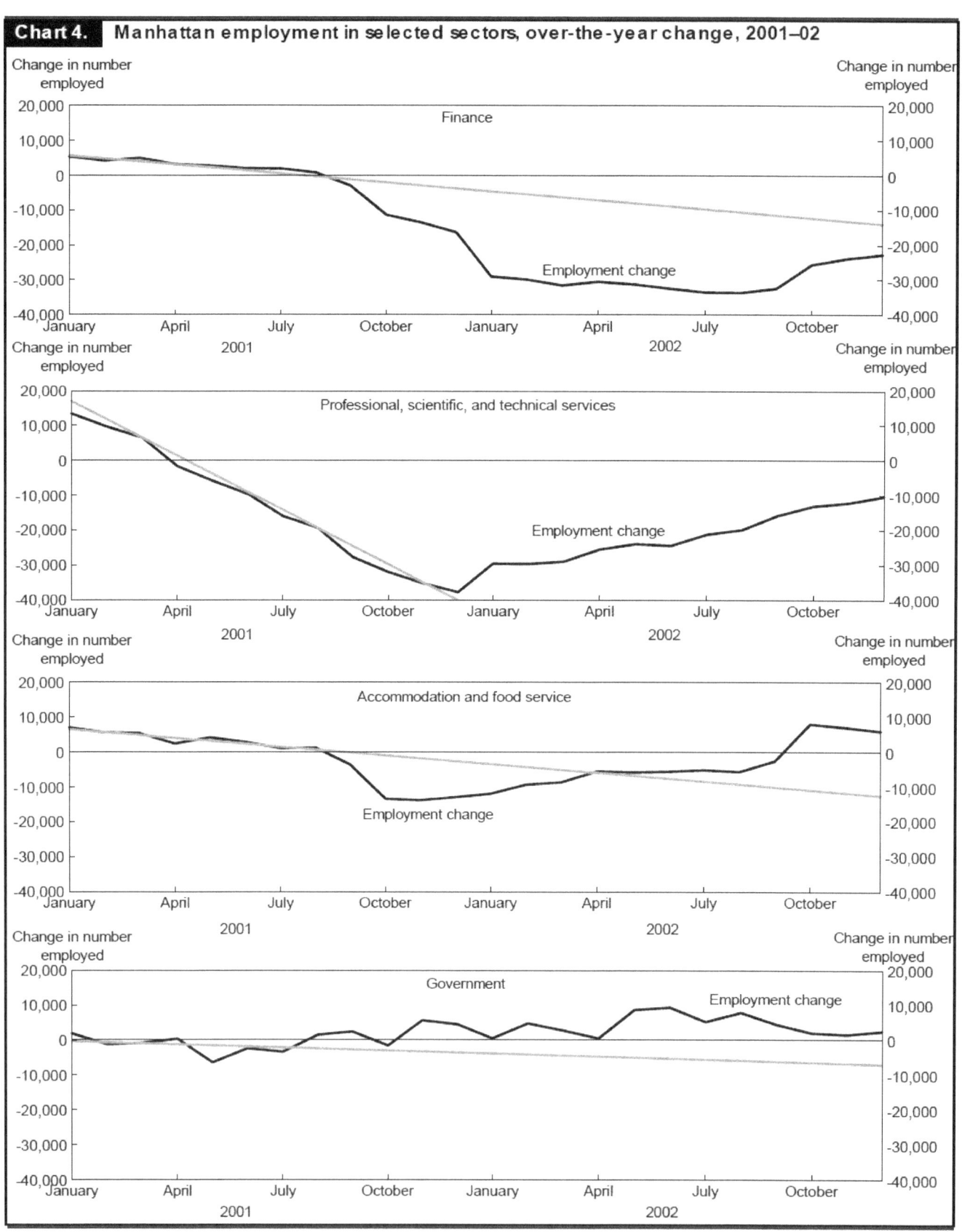

Chart 4. Manhattan employment in selected sectors, over-the-year change, 2001–02

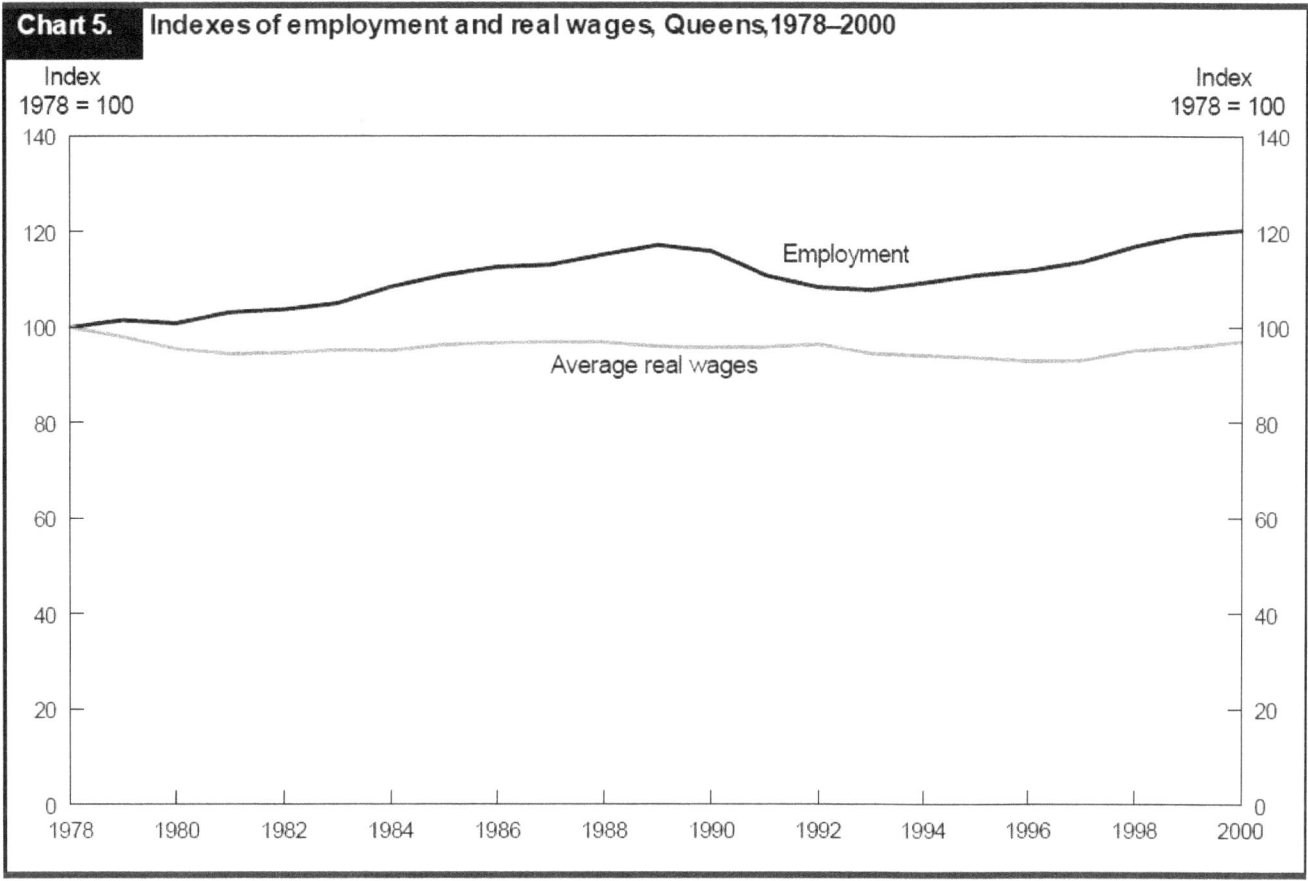

Chart 5. Indexes of employment and real wages, Queens, 1978–2000

Index
1978 = 100

Employment

Average real wages

With the notable exception of scheduled air transportation—a category within the transportation and warehouse sector—industries in Queens were less vulnerable than those in Manhattan to the economic effects of the national recession and the 9/11 terrorist attack. One possible explanation for this difference is that, in Queens, no single sector accounted for more than 20 percent of the total wage pool.

Queens has long been the home of a major league baseball franchise and, even longer, of the U. S. Tennis Open, both of which contribute to an average wage of $71,075 in spectator sports, a category within the arts, entertainment, and recreation sector. This high average wage helped raise the average wage for the entire sector.

Finance and insurance, though not a dominant sector in the Queens economy in terms of jobs, recorded the highest published average sector wage: $55,760, an amount 59.4 percent higher than the average borough wage. Banking accounted for much more of the sector's employment in Queens than in securities-dominated Manhattan. The average wage in Queens for the category of securities and commodity contract brokerage, within the finance and insurance sector, was $86,000, 67.2 percent lower than the average wage for the same category in Manhattan. The highest-paying detailed

industry category in Queens was in the information sector.

By 2002, two dynamics had taken place in the labor market economy in Queens. The first was in jobs, as average monthly employment dropped by 9,376, or 2.0 percent. The second was in average wages, which had risen 7.6 percent, or $2,652. During the 2-year period from 2000 to 2002, the borough experienced a marginal increase in population, attributed, as noted, to immigration. Table 7 gives an overview of the job situation, population, and wages in Queens in 2002.

The increase in average wages was shared across all sectors except accommodation and food services, which recorded a 3.3-percent decline. Once more unlike the situation in Manhattan, where total wages had declined, total wages in Queens increased 5.5 percent during the 2-year period. Table 8 shows the employment and wage situation for the various sectors of the Queens economy in 2002.

Transportation and warehousing. The transportation and warehousing sector represented 13.0 percent of the borough's employment base. Within the sector, two categories—scheduled air transportation and support activities for air transportation—accounted for 45.0 percent of all sector

Table 7. Trends in jobs, population, and wages, Queens, 2000 and 2002

Category	Number or amount	
	2000	2002
Total jobs	480,676	471,376
Total population	2,229,379	2,237,815
Total wages	$16,816,744,366	$17,738,593,994
Average wage	$34,986	$37,638

SOURCES: Job and wage data—BLS QCEW program; population data—U.S. Census Bureau website http://eire.census.gov/popest/data/counties/CO-EST2003-01php (visited April 2003).

jobs and 52.4 percent of all sector wages.

From 2000 to 2002, 7,353 jobs in scheduled air transportation (25.8 percent of all jobs in the category) were eliminated. The loss represented 78.4 percent of all jobs lost in Queens over the period, while average wages in the category rose 18.4 percent, to $63,682. During the same period, support activities for air transportation lost 266 jobs (4.0 percent of all jobs in the category).

Health care and social assistance.   Health care and social assistance (17.7 percent of Queens employment) experienced a 2.7-percent increase in average monthly employment between 2000 and 2002.

Construction.   In 2002, 37.5 percent of all New York City construction jobs were located in Queens; however, the sector accounted for only 8.9 percent of the borough's employment base.

Retail trade.   With 10.4 percent of Queens' employment base in retail trade (49,019 jobs), the sector is an important

Table 8. Employment and wages in selected sectors, Queens, 2000 and 2002

Sector	Average monthly employment	Percent of Queens employment	Total wages	Percent of total Queens wages	Average wage
2000					
Queens[1]	480,676	100.00	$16,816,744,366	100.00	$34,986
Finance and insurance	12,112	2.52	675,371,016	4.02	55,760
Professional, scientific, and technical	10,476	2.18	378,915,871	2.25	36,170
Information	10,663	2.22	494,792,260	2.94	46,402
Arts, entertainment, and recreation	4,513	.94	190,237,246	1.13	42,152
Management of companies	1,713	.36	95,183,148	.57	55,552
Real estate, and rental and leasing	14,864	3.09	484,378,171	2.88	32,587
Manufacturing	46,504	9.67	1,484,632,976	8.83	31,925
Administrative and support, and waste	22,876	4.76	582,435,487	3.46	25,460
Construction	39,876	8.30	2,026,803,620	12.05	50,828
Wholesale trade	24,580	5.11	1,011,667,221	6.02	41,159
Retail trade	50,617	10.53	1,110,824,989	6.61	21,946
Transportation and warehousing	71,717	14.92	3,060,042,232	18.20	42,668
Educational services	17,612	3.66	562,436,754	3.34	31,935
Health care and social assistance	92,706	19.29	3,090,042,496	18.37	33,332
Accommodation and food services	26,429	5.50	458,553,390	2.73	17,350
Other services	20,937	4.36	452,676,755	2.69	21,621
Government	8,594	1.79	457,823,244	2.72	53,276
Unclassified	1,511	.31	26,223,372	.16	17,356
2002					
Queens[1]	471,300	100.00	17,738,593,994	100.00	37,638
Finance and insurance	13,037	2.77	868,029,750	4.89	66,583
Professional, scientific, and technical	10,338	2.19	406,879,776	2.29	39,358
Information	10,233	2.17	495,871,983	2.80	48,459
Arts, entertainment, and recreation	4,381	.93	194,480,208	1.10	44,388
Management of companies	1,767	.37	106,447,472	.60	60,245
Real estate, and rental and leasing	14,773	3.13	511,118,040	2.88	34,598
Manufacturing	39,277	8.33	1,376,590,867	7.76	35,049
Administrative and support, and waste	24,340	5.16	631,393,369	3.56	25,940
Construction	41,906	8.89	2,316,260,977	13.06	55,273
Wholesale trade	23,906	5.07	1,067,495,199	6.02	44,653
Retail trade	49,019	10.40	1,139,265,616	6.42	23,241
Transportation and warehousing	61,273	13.00	2,867,920,008	16.17	46,806
Educational services	18,379	3.90	629,567,893	3.55	34,255
Health care and social assistance	95,213	20.20	3,440,285,442	19.39	36,133
Accommodation and food services	28,523	6.05	478,329,315	2.70	16,770
Other services	20,695	4.39	484,821,444	2.73	23,427
Government	7,600	1.61	450,379,581	2.54	59,257
Unclassified	4,125	.88	82,016,747	.46	19,885

[1] Detailed entries do not necessarily sum to totals. (See appendix.)   SOURCE: BLS QCEW program.

component of the borough's economy. Within the period from 2000 to 2002, jobs in retail trade declined 3.2 percent, while average wages increased 5.9 percent, to $23,241.

Manufacturing. Within New York City, 28.3 percent (39,277) of all manufacturing jobs were located in Queens. However, the sector accounted for only 8.3 percent of the borough's employment base.

"Local" and "export" economies. In Queens, the local economy is the driving economic force. This group of industries comprised 316,193 jobs, or 67.1 percent of all jobs in Queens in 2002. Jobs had increased by 2.6 percent, or 8,098, over 2000. By contrast, the export industries, which accounted for 155,079 jobs in 2002, saw a decline of 10.1 percent from 2000, a loss of 17,465 jobs. In 2002, the average wage of export jobs was $44,025, 27.6 percent higher than the $34,506 average for "local"-sector jobs.

A trend-line analysis suggests that the terrorist attack of 9/11 had a significant effect on the Queens labor market economy. What most likely would have been a relatively mild turndown attributable to the national recession became a deeper decline due to 9/11.

The overall effect of 9/11 extended for 9 months (September through June; see chart 6), with the trough arriving during December 2001. The Queens economy began to lose jobs in September 2001, and the losses extended through November 2002, a 14-month period. A breakdown of specific key sectors, given in table 9, points out the differing effects of 9/11, in terms of lost jobs and lost wages, on the Queens economy.

The transportation and warehousing industry, which might be considered part of the "export" economy in Queens because of the dominance of the two airports, lost 112,000 job months and $435,139,559 in wages, while some sectors were adding jobs during the entire period. Also, with the high concentration of hotels and motels at the airports, it may be that some losses in accommodation and food services jobs were due to the terrorist attack and the subsequent grounding of airplanes.[17]

The terrorist attack accounted for approximately 140,00 lost job months (the equivalent of 15,550 jobs each month for 9 months) and about half a billion dollars in lost wages. As in Manhattan, a single category—in the case of Queens, air transportation—was the driving force in the downturn in the

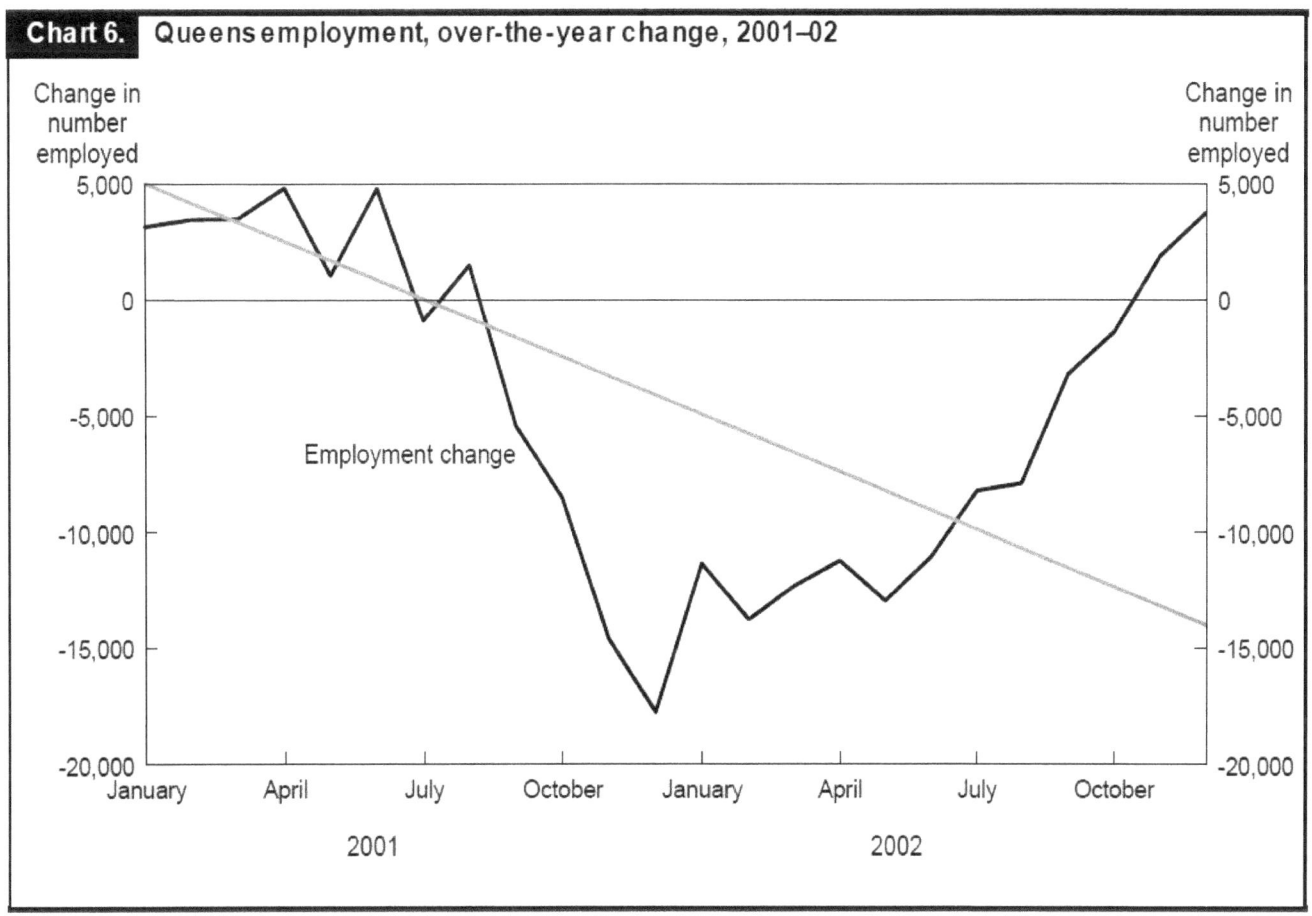

Chart 6. Queens employment, over-the-year change, 2001–02

Table 9. Effect of 9/11 in job months and lost or gained wages over the 2000–02 period, Queens

Sector	Job months	Wages, lost or gained
Total lost	−139,835	−$511,312,290
Professional, scientific, and technical	−1,800	−5,808,389
Arts, entertainment, and recreation	−1,800	−6,512,694
Management of companies	−450	−2,112,176
Manufacturing	−5,250	−14,943,909
Administrative and support, and waste	−1,500	−3,206,716
Construction	−4,000	−18,191,468
Wholesale trade	−75	−268,137
Retail trade	−6,400	−12,262,171
Transportation and warehousing	−112,000	−435,139,559
Air transportation	−89,000	−400,704,862
Educational services	−2,400	−6,573,099
Accommodation and food services	−3,600	−5,255,148
Other services	−560	−1,038,824
Total gained[1]	30,300	140,233,479
Finance and insurance	9,000	50,157,865
Information	6,000	23,781,709
Health care and social assistance	5,200	15,150,528
Government	10,000	50,510,939

[1] Detailed entries do not necessarily sum to totals. (See appendix.)   SOURCE: BLS QCEW program.

borough's economy. Air transportation contributed 63.7 percent of all lost job months and 78.4 percent of all lost wages in Queens that were associated with the terrorist attacks.

Brooklyn

With its 2000 population of 2,465,326, Brooklyn would rank as the fourth-largest city in the United States were it independently incorporated. In 2000, the borough was in the midst of one of the most substantial periods of sustained job growth during the past 50 years. In the later portion of the 1990s, job increases were both marked and strong, reflecting the economic vitality experienced by both the Nation and the city. By 2000, the borough had reached the level of about 442,000 jobs, the highest job total attained since 1978.

Although the Brooklyn economy was creating new jobs, the wages associated with these new jobs had not demonstrated the same upward trend. Real wages in 2000, were, in fact, lower than they had been in 1978. (See chart 7.) In 2000, Brooklyn's average wage of $30,760 was 57.6 percent lower than Manhattan's and 12.1 percent lower than that of Queens.

After Queens, Brooklyn was the leading destination for new immigrants to New York City. Between 1990 and 1994 alone, nearly 200,000 immigrants moved to the borough, with nearly 25 percent (49,741) coming from the former Soviet Union.[18] Although often highly trained, these immigrants, like those settling in Queens, tended to be employed in low-paying jobs. Finally, Brooklyn is a borough of small businesses, with approximately 66 percent of the borough's business establishments employing fewer than five workers.[19]

The borough's 441,911 jobs (see table 10) represented 12.3 percent of the entire New York City job base in 2000. In terms of New York's employment mix, 26.3 percent of all city jobs in the health care and social assistance sector, and 20.8 percent of all city construction jobs were located in Brooklyn. Construction, however, accounted for only 5.5 percent of Brooklyn's total jobs.

Relatively few people living outside of New York City traveled to Brooklyn to work. The Brooklyn economy served, for the most part, the needs of its resident population. Fully 64.7 percent of Brooklyn workers were borough residents. Those living outside of New York City and working in Brooklyn accounted for just 11.4 percent of the borough's workforce, while those living in other New York City counties and working in Brooklyn composed 23.9 percent of the workforce.[20]

In looking at employment distribution in Brooklyn, two sectors stand out: health care and social assistance, with 30.6 percent of the borough's jobs, and retail trade, with 12.1 percent of the jobs. The prominence of these two sectors underscored the importance of the "local economy," which, in aggregate, accounted for 78.4 percent of Brooklyn's entire job base. This employment distribution pattern made Brooklyn less vulnerable than Manhattan to the effects of an economic turndown or a terrorist attack. However, it also contributed to the low average wages in the borough, compared with those in Manhattan and Queens. Table 11 presents various aspects of employment and wages for the sectors making up the Brooklyn economy in 2000.

Within sectors, there was none of the significant variation between wages and specific jobs that existed in Manhattan. Most Brooklyn jobs had wages between $20,000 and $50,000. In

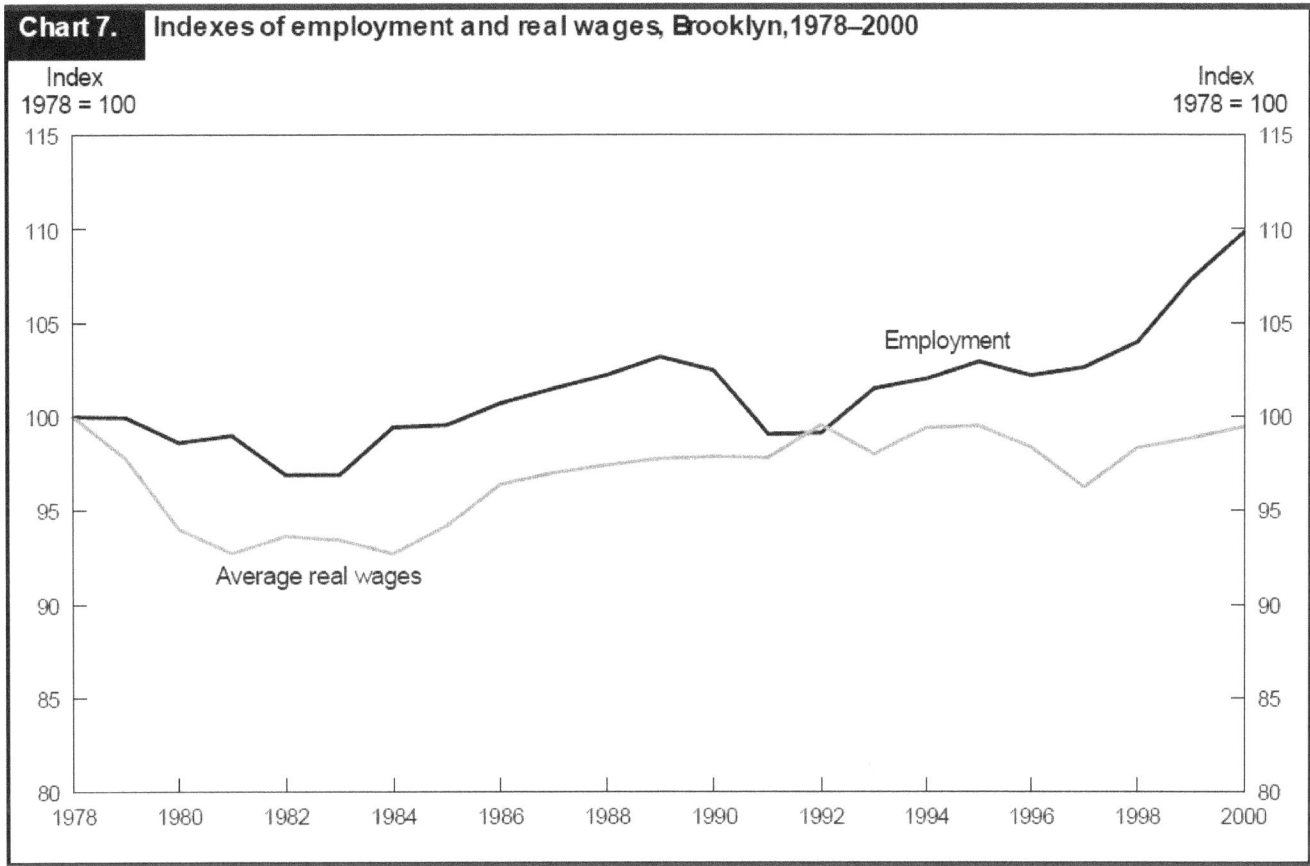

Chart 7. Indexes of employment and real wages, Brooklyn, 1978–2000

addition, representing 53,452 of the borough's jobs, the retail trade sector, with an average wage of $21,203, was typically among the lowest paying of any sector and pulled down the borough's average wage.

With the borough's economy "locally focused," Brooklyn's employment base changed relatively little between 2000 and 2002. At 1.0 percent, or 4,408 jobs, the loss of jobs over the 2-year period was marginal. However, within the same time frame, a different phenomenon was taking place in regard to wages. Unlike the situation during the 23-year period from 1978 to 2000, when real wages were stagnant, wage growth in Brooklyn between 2000 and 2002 was substantial. During the 2-year period, average wages advanced 7.0 percent, to $32,903 (see table 10), while aggregate borough wages increased 5.9 percent. The highest-paying detailed category was found in the transportation and warehousing sector.

Some volatility between sectors defined the labor market scene within the borough between the years 2000 and 2002. A sector-by-sector analysis affords an insight into these dynamics. Table 11 presents the employment and wage situation for the various sectors of the Brooklyn economy in 2002.

Health care and social assistance. With an employment base of 142,570 in 2002, this sector was clearly Brooklyn's largest employer. Within the 2-year period, jobs increased by 5.4 percent, while the average wage of the sector rose 10.1 percent, to $34,217, an amount 4.0 percent higher than the average borough wage.

Retail trade. With 12 percent of all borough jobs in 2002, the retail trade sector was Brooklyn's second-largest employer. Although jobs in the sector declined 1.7 percent between 2000 and 2002, to 52,527, average sector wages rose 11.0 percent within the same period, to $23,540. This general trend of job losses and average wage gains was replicated throughout all sectors.

Manufacturing. One in 4 (25.7 percent) of all city manufacturing jobs was located in Brooklyn. The manufacturing sector represented 8.1 percent of Brooklyn's job base, the third-largest employment sector within the borough.

As with Queens, the apparel industry was the largest employer in the sector. Cut-and-sew apparel manufacturing represented 19.4 percent of all manufacturing jobs. Between 2000 and 2002,

Table 10.	Trends in jobs, population, and wages, Brooklyn, 2000 and 2002	
Category	Number or amount	
	2000	2002
Total jobs	441,911	437,503
Total population	2,465,326	2,488,194
Total wages	$13,593,175,787	$14,395,292,151
Average wage	$30,760	$32,903

SOURCES: Job and wage data—BLS QCEW program; population data—U.S. Census Bureau website **http://eire.census.gov/popest/data/counties/CO-EST2003-01php** (visited April 2003).

jobs in the sector decreased 32.0 percent, to 6,906, while wages increased 3.6 percent, to $13,902.

Construction. The construction sector accounted for 5.0 percent of all borough jobs in 2002. Within the 2-year period, jobs decreased 10.1 percent, to 21,876, while average wages increased 7.0 percent, to $44,098.

Educational services. The educational services sector accounted for 6.0 percent of all Brooklyn jobs in 2002. With 2000 as the base, jobs within this sector increased 11.2 percent (by 2,652), while average wages declined 2.9 percent, to $36,758. This large increase in educational service sector jobs helped minimize the effect of the 2-year total job loss of 4,408, which characterized the entire Brooklyn labor market economy.

Table 11.	Employment and wages in selected sectors, Brooklyn, 2000 and 2002				
Sector	Average monthly employment	Percent of Brooklyn employment	Total wages	Percent of total Brooklyn wages	Average wage
2000					
Brooklyn[1]	441,911	100.00	$13,593,175,787	100.00	$30,760
Finance and insurance	14,197	3.21	767,744,135	5.65	54,078
Professional, scientific, and technical	11,523	2.61	454,271,104	3.34	39,422
Information	8,627	1.95	416,804,663	3.07	48,314
Arts, entertainment, and recreation	3,509	.79	87,364,935	.64	24,896
Management of companies	944	.21	40,937,754	.30	43,385
Real estate, and rental and leasing	13,581	3.07	376,387,244	2.77	27,715
Manufacturing	43,212	9.78	1,157,617,214	8.52	26,789
Administrative and support, and waste	18,157	4.11	407,609,949	3.00	22,449
Construction	24,325	5.50	1,002,449,127	7.37	41,210
Wholesale trade	23,868	5.40	809,424,521	5.95	33,912
Retail trade	53,452	12.10	1,133,311,085	8.34	21,203
Transportation and warehousing	18,811	4.26	605,890,398	4.46	32,210
Educational services	22,591	5.34	893,340,674	8.57	37,868
Health care and social assistance	135,238	30.60	4,202,539,509	30.92	31,075
Accommodation and food services	16,894	3.82	245,727,434	1.81	14,545
Other services	19,951	4.51	394,377,201	2.90	19,768
Government	5,565	1.26	255,972,677	1.88	45,997
Unclassified	1,823	.41	30,346,729	.22	16,650
2002					
Brooklyn[1]	437,503	100.00	14,395,292,151	100.00	32,903
Finance and insurance	14,179	3.24	833,158,569	5.79	58,760
Professional, scientific, and technical	11,570	2.64	479,085,151	3.33	41,407
Information	7,776	1.78	372,352,812	2.59	47,886
Arts, entertainment, and recreation	3,546	.81	94,322,774	.66	26,600
Management of companies	1,088	.25	49,836,824	.35	45,799
Real estate, and rental and leasing	13,457	3.08	391,182,563	2.72	29,069
Manufacturing	35,546	8.12	1,058,185,258	7.35	29,770
Administrative and support, and waste	18,244	4.17	413,072,408	2.87	22,642
Construction	21,876	5.00	964,668,126	6.70	44,098
Wholesale trade	21,498	4.91	770,452,261	5.35	35,839
Retail trade	52,525	12.01	1,236,452,071	8.59	23,540
Transportation and warehousing	18,036	4.12	621,729,059	4.32	34,471
Educational services	26,243	6.00	964,637,832	6.70	36,758
Health care and social assistance	142,570	32.59	4,878,306,296	33.89	34,217
Accommodation and food services	17,464	3.99	268,251,315	1.86	15,361
Other services	20,005	4.57	423,744,669	2.94	21,182
Government	3,505	.80	191,122,197	1.33	54,531
Unclassified	4,388	1.00	91,760,284	.64	20,910

[1] Detailed entries do not necessarily sum to totals. (See appendix.)   SOURCE: BLS QCEW program.

Administrative and support, and waste. Within this sector, the number of jobs (17,280) and the average wage ($22,497) remained relatively constant from 2000 to 2002. However, during the same period, the category of employment services, which accounted for 35.9 percent of the sector's jobs, demonstrated explosive job growth: 23.2 percent, or 1,511 jobs. Average wages in the category increased 19.8 percent, to $20,397, during the same period.

"Local" and "export" economy. As noted earlier, the "local economy" sector was the borough's economic driving force. This sector was composed of 350,271 jobs (80.1 percent of all Brooklyn jobs) in 2002, an increase of 1.2 percent (4,020 jobs), over the 2000 figure. By contrast, the "export economy" sector accounted for just 87,162 jobs (19.9 percent), a decrease of 8.8 percent (8,431 jobs), during the same period.

However, in 2002, the average wage in the "export" sector, $37,610, was 18.5 percent higher than the average wage of $31,734 for "local" sector jobs. This differential underscored the broader influence of "export" sector jobs.

Using the trend-line methodology to analyze the Brooklyn labor market economy in the aggregate suggests that the terrorist attack of 9/11 had a distinct effect that was independent of the national recession. Though clearly not as intense as that experienced in Manhattan and Queens, this effect altered Brooklyn's employment pattern for some time. (See chart 8.)

The disruption, which began after September 2001, lasted for 2 months, until November 2001. It exerted two distinct influences, the same as affected the Manhattan economy. First, the economic downturn in Brooklyn was deeper than would have been expected just from the recession. Second, the trough of the recession occurred earlier, in October 2001, than would have been anticipated. (Chart 8 brings out both of these points.)

In tracing the economic downturn in Brooklyn, one sees a pattern emerge. Job losses began in April 2001, 3 months after the start of the recession in the city, and lasted until September 2002. In August 2001, it appeared that the borough might experience positive job growth. However, as the chart points out, at that time a sharp and marked economic decline overtook Brooklyn. The falloff was attributable, in large measure, to the terrorist attack of 9/11, which helped fuel a significant downturn in employment. (Note that the sharp declines in employment recorded during April, May, and June were related to specific events in the government, health care, and transportation and warehouse sectors.)

Chart 9 demonstrates that the "export" sector of the Brooklyn economy was the driving force of the economic turndown in the borough and also points out a clear 9/11 effect: the sector, which was losing jobs in January 2001, experienced a marked and prolonged downturn after September 2001. The terrorist attack accounted for 27,220 lost job months (the equivalent of 9,100 jobs each month for 3 months) and $64,776,315 in lost wages. (See table 12.)

Unlike the situation in Manhattan and Queens, where single job categories—that is, finance and air transportation, were the driving forces in the economic downturns, in Brooklyn the overall effect was influenced by multiple sectors and job categories. Overall, compared with its effect on Manhattan and Queens, the effect of the terrorist attack on Brooklyn's economy was less intense. However, it was distinct and measurable.

The Bronx

As the year 2000 began, the Bronx economy was in its 8th year of expansion. The job count had reached a level of 213,107, the highest number of jobs since 1978, and it was still climbing. Mirroring the pattern for the country, this increase in jobs was accompanied by an increase in real wages. Chart 10 shows the trend in these two economic variables from 1978 to 2000.

The borough's 213,107 jobs (see table 13) represented 5.9 percent of all of the jobs in New York City. In terms of employment mix, 15.6 percent of all city jobs in health care and social assistance were located in the Bronx. This sector alone represented 37.6 percent of all jobs in the borough.

With its 2000 population of 1,332,650 (see table 13), the Bronx was the city's fourth-largest borough. The employment-residence distribution pattern was similar to that recorded for Queens and Brooklyn, with the overwhelming majority of Bronx workers living either in the Bronx or in other city boroughs. Specifically, 60.1 percent of the Bronx workforce resided in the borough, 18.4 percent called other New York City counties home, and 21.5 percent lived outside of the city.[21]

As regards employment distribution in the Bronx, three sectors—health care and social assistance (37.7 percent), retail trade (10.5 percent), and educational services (7.4 percent)—represented 55.6 percent of all Bronx jobs. The borough's average salary of $32,831 was 6.7 percent higher than that of Brooklyn, and 6.2 percent lower than that of Queens, in 2000. As noted earlier, the Bronx's "hometown" industry is health care, and just as Wall Street influences Manhattan's economic well-being, the fortunes of health care determine the economic health of the Bronx.

In 2000, 33.9 percent of all borough wages was generated by the health care industry alone (not including the social assistance industry). The industry's average wage of $39,298 was 19.6 percent higher than the average borough wage, but 16.5 percent lower than the comparable health care wage in Manhattan ($47,062.)

In the Bronx, the highest-paying published sector was arts, entertainment, and recreation. However, the sector's average wage of $66,384 (see table 14) was skewed by the presence of a major league sports franchise. Within sectors (excluding the arts, entertainment, and recreation sector), the two categories with the

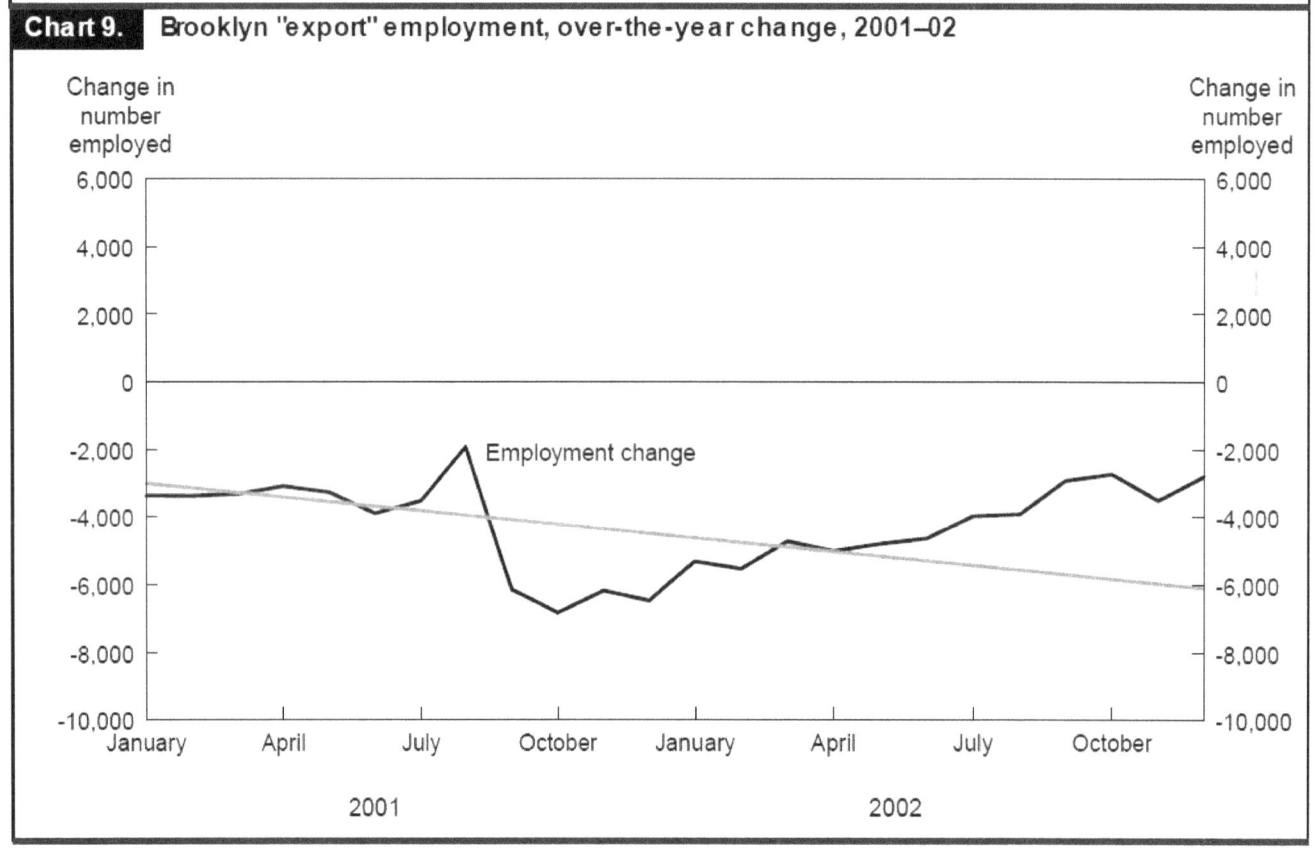

Chart 8. Brooklyn employment, over-the-year change, 2001–02

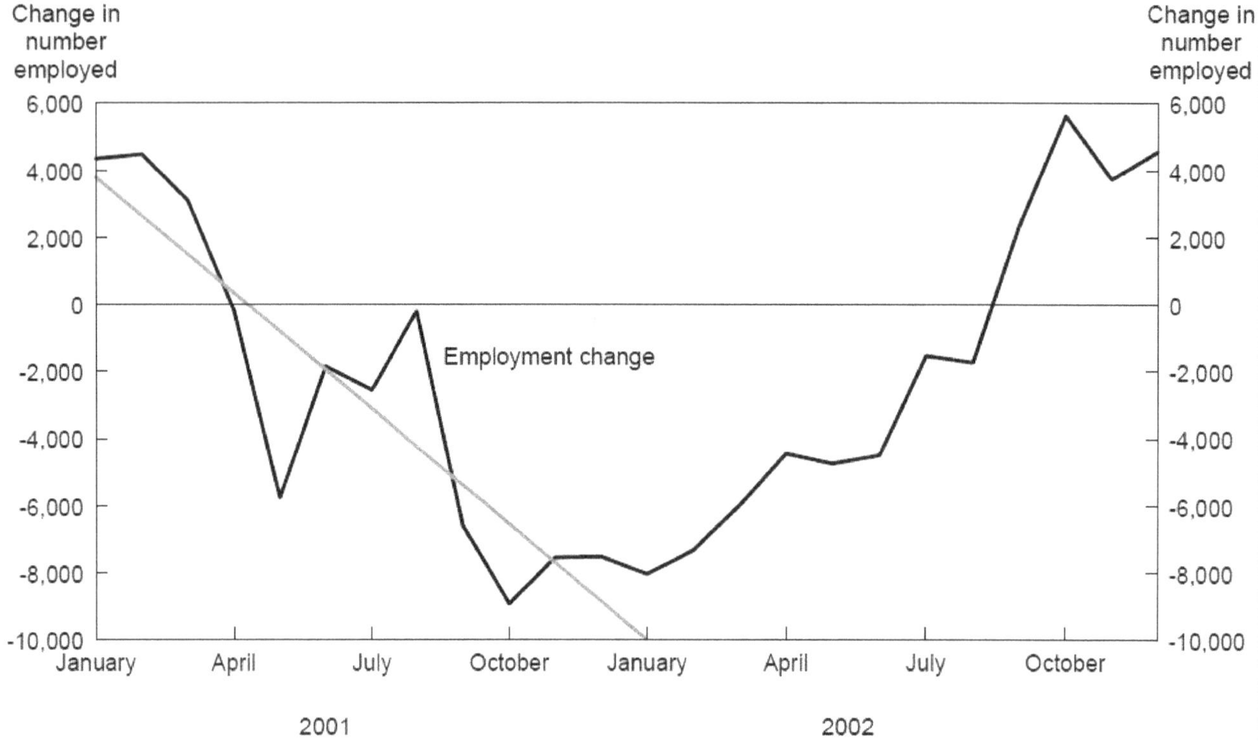

Chart 9. Brooklyn "export" employment, over-the-year change, 2001–02

Table 12. **Effect of 9/11 in job months and lost or gained wages, over the 2000–02 period, Brooklyn**

Sector	Job months	Wages, lost or gained
Total lost	−27,220	−$64,776,315
Professional, scientific, and technical	−1,050	−3,562,050
Arts, entertainment, and recreation	−1,200	−2,650,275
Real estate, and rental and leasing	−3,920	−9,393,040
Manufacturing	−1,800	−4,291,200
Administrative and support, and waste	−2,250	−4,218,750
Construction	−2,000	−7,108,000
Wholesale trade	−400	−1,162,400
Retail trade	−4,500	−8,531,500
Transportation and warehousing	−3,750	−10,484,850
Educational services	−1,750	−5,469,850
Accommodation and food services	−200	−248,400
Other services	−4,400	−7,656,000
Total gained	17,400	52,063,010
Finance and insurance	1,800	8,698,680
Management of companies	400	1,737,130
Health care and social assistance	15,200	41,627,200

¹ Detailed entries do not necessarily sum to totals. (See appendix.)   Source: BLS QCEW program.

highest average wage were in the information sector: data processing and related services, at $67,192, and wired telecommunications carriers, at $61,274.

In 2002, the Bronx labor market economy was unique in New York City: the borough was the only one in the city that recorded a growth in jobs over the 2000 job count. Over the 2-year period, average monthly employment rose 1.3 percent, or 2,857 jobs, while average wages rose 8.9 percent, or $2,933. Within the same time frame, the borough also experienced a marginal increase in population. Table 13 provides an overview of the job situation, population, and wages in the Bronx in 2002.

The increase in average wages was shared by all sectors, except professional, scientific, and technical occupations, which registered a 1.9-percent decline. Two sectors—administrative and support, and waste; and accommodation and food service—together accounted for an increase of 1,985 jobs, or 66.6 percent of the entire 2-year job gain.

An analysis of selected sectors, for which various employment and wage figures are shown in table 14, provides deeper insights into the Bronx labor market economy.

Health care and social assistance. In this dominant sector of the Bronx economy, the two categories of general medical and surgical hospitals (36.8 percent) and nursing care facilities (17.8 percent) accounted for a combined 54.6 percent of all sector jobs.

Manufacturing. In 2002, 6.9 percent of all manufacturing jobs in New York City were located in the Bronx, while the sector itself represented 4.5 percent of the borough's jobs. Between 2000 and 2002, the Bronx economy lost 1,348 manufacturing jobs, or 12.3 percent of the borough's manufacturing job base.

During the same period, average wages in the manufacturing sector increased 8.7 percent, to $34,138.

Educational services. With 16,240 jobs, the educational services sector was the borough's third-largest employment sector. Within the sector, almost half (47.8 percent) of the jobs were in the category of colleges and universities. Between 2000 and 2002, the number of jobs remained constant (7,762), while average wages rose 20.7 percent, to $37,159.

A trend-line analysis reveals that the terrorist attack of 9/11 did not exert any specific effect on the Bronx's labor market economy. Chart 11 indicates that a recordable economic downturn began in October 2001. However, the trend follows what would have been expected from the general economic decline.

The 2001 recession seems to have been mild in the Bronx, lasting for just 3 months—until January 2002—at which point the Bronx economy started to gain jobs again. However, dividing the Bronx into its "local economy" and "export economy" segments underscores some important relationships.

The "local economy" sector appears not to have been influenced by either the terrorist attack of 9/11 or the 2001 recession. Except for job losses occurring in May 2001, due to specific issues related to the health care sector, job growth in the Bronx began in June 2001 and continued until December 2002. (See chart 12, top panel.)

By contrast, the "export" sector of the Bronx economy was influenced both by the 2001 recession and by the terrorist attack of 9/11. An employment downturn commenced in February 2001 and lasted until October 2002, a period of 20 months. (See chart 12, bottom panel.)

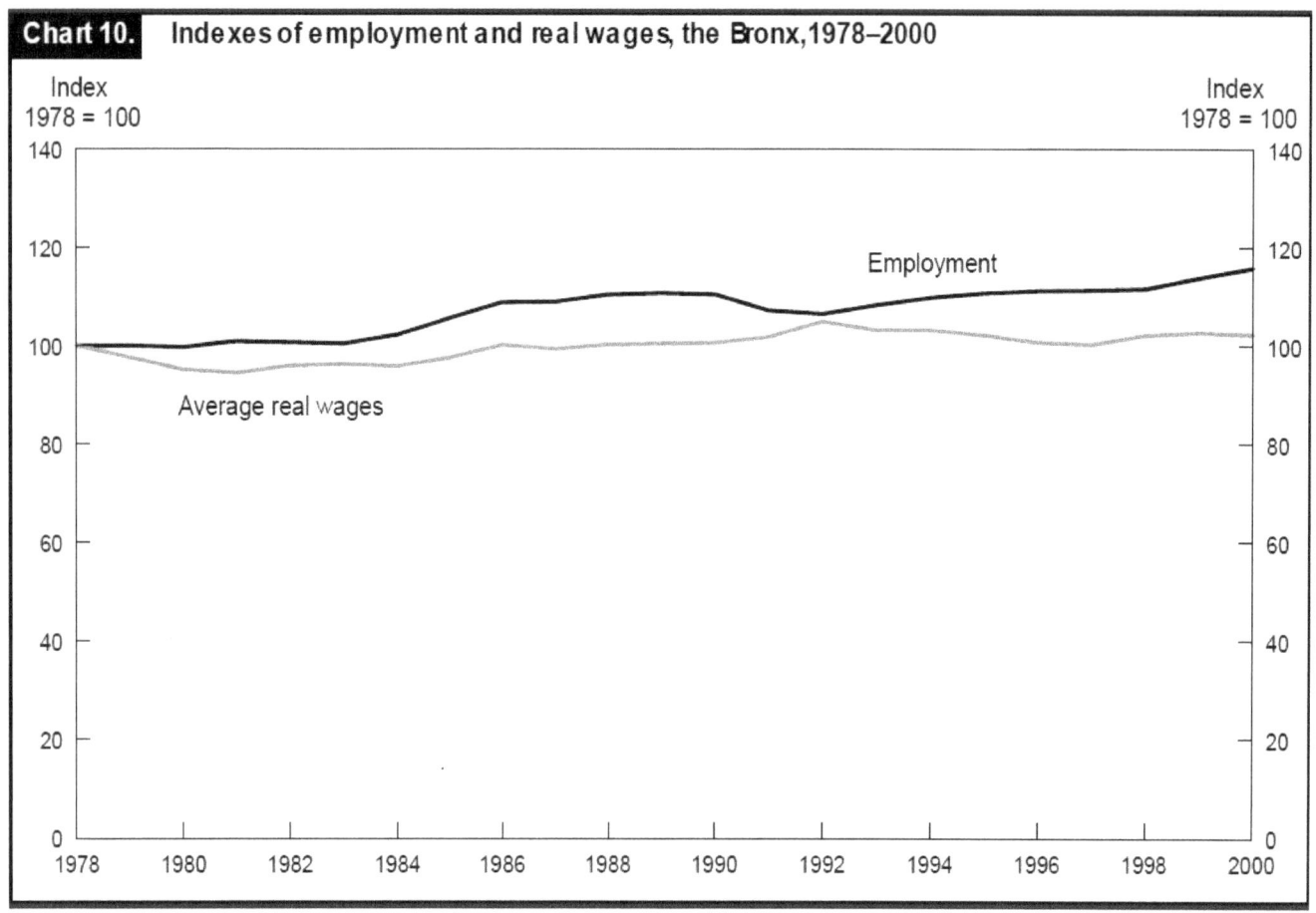

Chart 10. Indexes of employment and real wages, the Bronx, 1978–2000

Index
1978 = 100

Index
1978 = 100

The strength of the "local economy" in the Bronx overshadowed the influence of the "export economy" and explains why the effect of the terrorist attack of 9/11 was not readily apparent. It also points out why the 2001 recession was relatively mild in the Bronx. A sector-by-sector breakdown underscores the differing effects of 9/11, in terms of lost jobs and lost wages, on the Bronx economy. The terrorist attack accounted for about 20,000 lost job months (the equivalent of 5,000 jobs each month for 4 months) and approximately $53 million in lost wages. (See table 15.)

Staten Island

For Staten Island, the 1990s was a decade of vigorous job growth. Commencing in 1992, the borough participated in the economic expansion that enveloped the Nation. By the year 2000, Staten Island had reached a level of 88,243 jobs, just shy of the 24-year high recorded in 2001 (88,289 jobs). A sustained growth in real wages that began in 1998 accompanied the borough's increase in employment. Chart 13 shows the trend in employment and real wages for Staten Island from 1978 to 2000. With a 2000 population of 443,728 (see table 16), the borough was New

York's smallest, and its 88,243 jobs represented just 2.5 percent of the city's job base.

Of all New York City boroughs, Staten Island was the one with the highest percentage of its workforce living within its borders (71.7 percent). Just 16.2 percent resided in other New York City counties, and 12.1 percent lived outside of the city. [22] As in Brooklyn and the Bronx, the Staten Island economy was primarily "local" in nature, serving, for the most part, the needs of its residents. Specifically, 85.9 percent of all Staten Island

Table 13. Trends in jobs, population, and wages, the Bronx, 2000 and 2002

Category	Number or amount	
	2000	2002
Total jobs	213,107	213,107
Total population	1,332,650	1,332,650
Total wages	$6,996,476,345	$6,996,476,345
Average wage	$32,831	$32,831

SOURCES: Job and wage data—BLS QCEW program; population data—U.S. Census Bureau website **http://eire.census.gov/popest/data/counties/CO-EST2003-01php** (visited April 2003).

Table 14. Employment and wages in selected sectors, the Bronx, 2000 and 2002

Sector	Average monthly employment	Percent of Bronx employment	Total wages	Percent of total Bronx wages	Average wage
2000					
The Bronx[1]	213,107	100.00	$6,996,476,345	100.00	$32,831
Finance and insurance	2,757	1.29	93,931,543	1.34	34,072
Professional, scientific, and technical	2,959	1.39	104,968,457	1.50	35,472
Information	4,340	2.04	194,664,015	2.78	44,853
Arts, entertainment, and recreation	2,930	1.37	194,476,423	2.78	66,384
Management of companies	1,172	.55	53,384,782	.76	45,537
Real estate, and rental and leasing	10,425	4.89	277,019,523	3.96	26,572
Manufacturing	10,969	5.15	344,465,227	4.92	31,403
Administrative and support, and waste	6,914	3.24	153,425,550	2.19	22,190
Construction	10,791	5.06	507,579,927	7.25	47,039
Wholesale trade	10,318	4.84	435,677,770	6.23	42,225
Retail trade	22,286	10.46	467,778,601	6.69	20,990
Transportation and warehousing	6,895	3.24	248,375,007	3.55	36,022
Educational services	15,692	7.36	474,712,590	6.79	30,251
Health care and social assistance	80,222	37.64	2,783,263,791	39.78	34,695
Accommodation and food services	9,409	4.42	125,659,269	1.80	13,355
Other services	7,943	3.73	167,592,483	2.40	21,100
Government	5,036	2.36	248,145,270	3.55	49,271
Unclassified	456	.21	7,113,394	.10	15,617
2002					
The Bronx[1]	215,964	100.00	7,723,770,707	100.00	35,764
Finance and insurance	2,881	1.33	101,206,081	1.31	35,134
Professional, scientific, and technical	3,180	1.47	110,656,135	1.43	34,794
Information	4,351	2.01	213,373,411	2.76	49,035
Arts, entertainment, and recreation	3,172	1.47	233,253,713	3.02	73,531
Management of companies	923	.43	44,939,406	.58	48,693
Real estate, and rental and leasing	10,107	4.68	285,202,168	3.69	28,217
Manufacturing	9,621	4.45	328,434,629	4.25	34,138
Administrative and support, and waste	8,113	3.76	195,221,576	2.53	24,064
Construction	9,762	4.52	480,536,174	6.22	49,228
Wholesale trade	9,956	4.61	445,121,055	5.76	44,708
Retail trade	22,653	10.49	523,325,794	6.78	23,101
Transportation and warehousing	6,773	3.14	258,200,958	3.34	38,124
Educational services	16,240	7.52	555,230,746	7.19	34,189
Health care and social assistance	80,573	37.31	3,055,312,035	39.56	37,920
Accommodation and food services	10,195	4.72	144,053,003	1.87	14,130
Other services	7,620	3.53	167,555,092	2.17	21,988
Government	6,867	3.18	430,899,955	5.58	62,749
Unclassified	1,299	.60	24,868,134	.32	19,143

[1] Detailed entries do not necessarily sum to totals. (See appendix.)   Source: BLS QCEW program.

jobs (75,764 jobs) in 2000 were associated with the "local economy." A look at employment distribution in Staten Island readily reveals that four sectors—health care and social assistance (30.1 percent), retail trade (16.6 percent), construction (7.6 percent), and accommodation and food service (6.1 percent)—accounted for 60.4 percent of all jobs and 55.6 percent of all wages. (See table 17.)

In terms of the number of jobs, the Staten Island economy peaked in 2001 and began to decline slightly in 2002. Between 2000 and 2002, the borough lost 754 jobs, or less than 1 percent of its job base. This small percentage loss underscored the buffering effect exerted by the "local economy." However, a different trend was being recorded in terms of average wages, which increased 5.7 percent, to $33,970, during the same 2-year period. (See table 16.) The increase in average wages was shared across all sectors except the information sector and the administrative and support, and waste sector, which recorded a 1.0-percent decline and an 8.7-percent drop, respectively.

During the 2-year period from 2000 to 2002, Staten Island's population increased 3.1 percent, the largest rate recorded within all of New York City. A selected sector-by-sector analysis affords greater insights. Table 17 gives a breakdown of various aspects of employment and wages associated with the different sectors of the Staten Island economy in 2002.

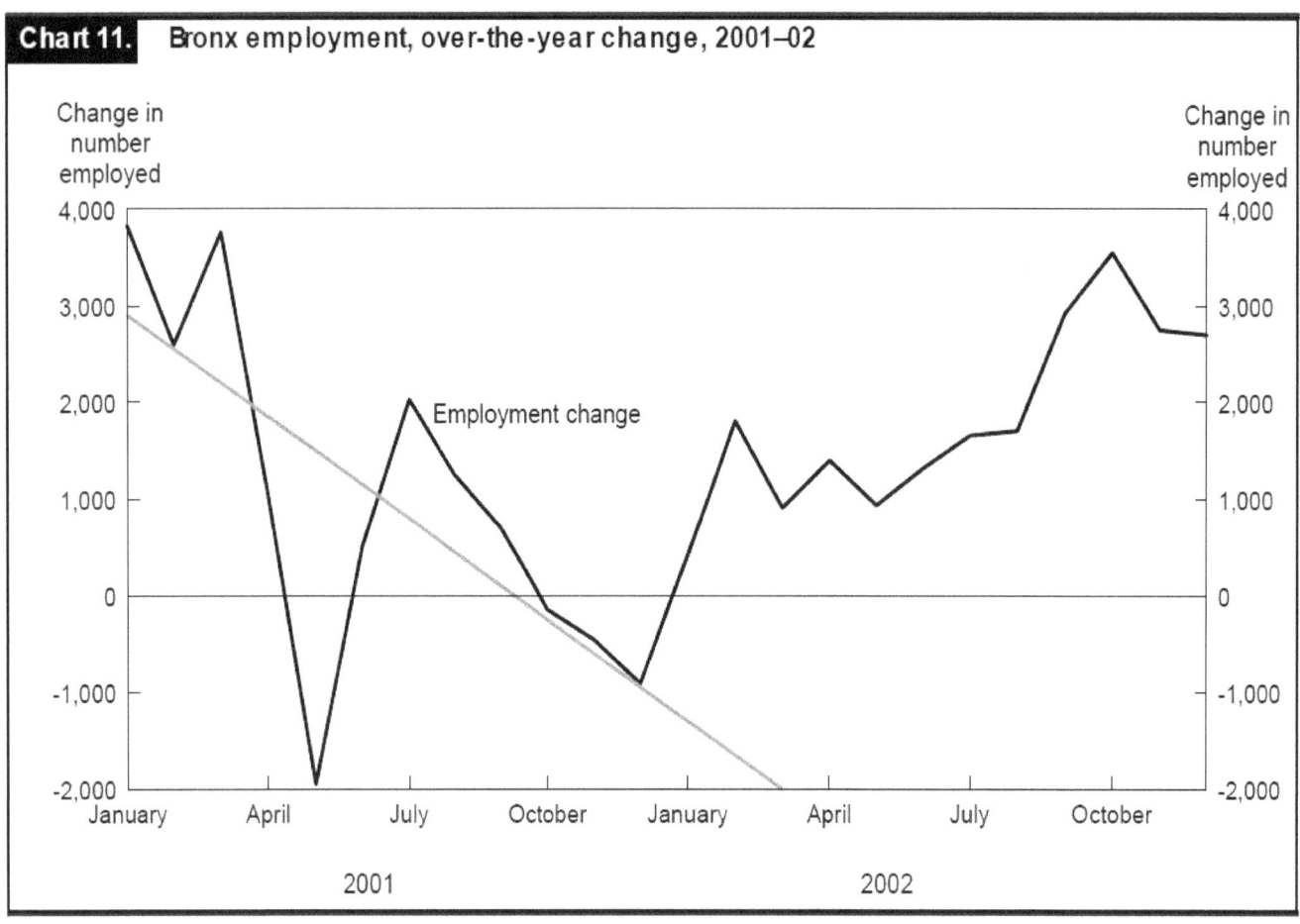

Chart 11. Bronx employment, over-the-year change, 2001–02

Health care and social assistance. As in Queens, Brooklyn, and the Bronx, this sector is Staten Island's largest employer, in terms of both jobs and total wages. In 2002, 5.0 percent of all New York City jobs in health care and social assistance were located in Staten Island.

Retail trade. The retail trade sector was the second-largest employment sector in Staten Island in terms of jobs and total wages. As regards the New York City economy, 5.5 percent of all jobs in retail trade were located in Staten Island.

Information. The information sector made up only 3.3 percent of all Staten Island jobs in 2002, but these 2,907 jobs represented a 13.0-percent decrease, or 433 jobs, from the number of jobs the borough had in 2000. This job loss alone accounted for 57.4 percent of all of the jobs lost in Staten Island between 2000 and 2002.

"Local" and "export" economy. The "export economy" sector represented just 14.1 percent of all Staten Island jobs

in 2002. During the period from 2000 to 2002, total jobs in this sector declined 1.9 percent, to 12,247, while total wages increased 1.1 percent, to $507,012,284, and the average wage increased 3.9 percent, to $39,942.

Within the "local economy" sector, a different pattern emerged. Jobs remained relatively constant between 2000 and 2002 (75,764 jobs), while total wages increased 5.6 percent, to $2,425,238,309; and the average wage increased 6.3 percent, to $32,761. The average "local economy" wage was 26.4 percent lower than that for the "export economy."

A trend-line analysis indicates that the terrorist attack of 9/11 exerted just a slight effect on the Staten Island labor market economy. The economic downturn that began in June 2001 was mostly a result of the national recession. The borough's recession bottomed out in January 2002, but job losses were still being recorded in December 2002. (See chart 14.)

The curve of the "local economy," shown in chart 15, mirrors somewhat that recorded for Staten Island as a whole. Job losses began in May 2001 and continued for 13 months, until June 2002, when the "local economy" began to add jobs.

As previously noted, job losses associated with the "export

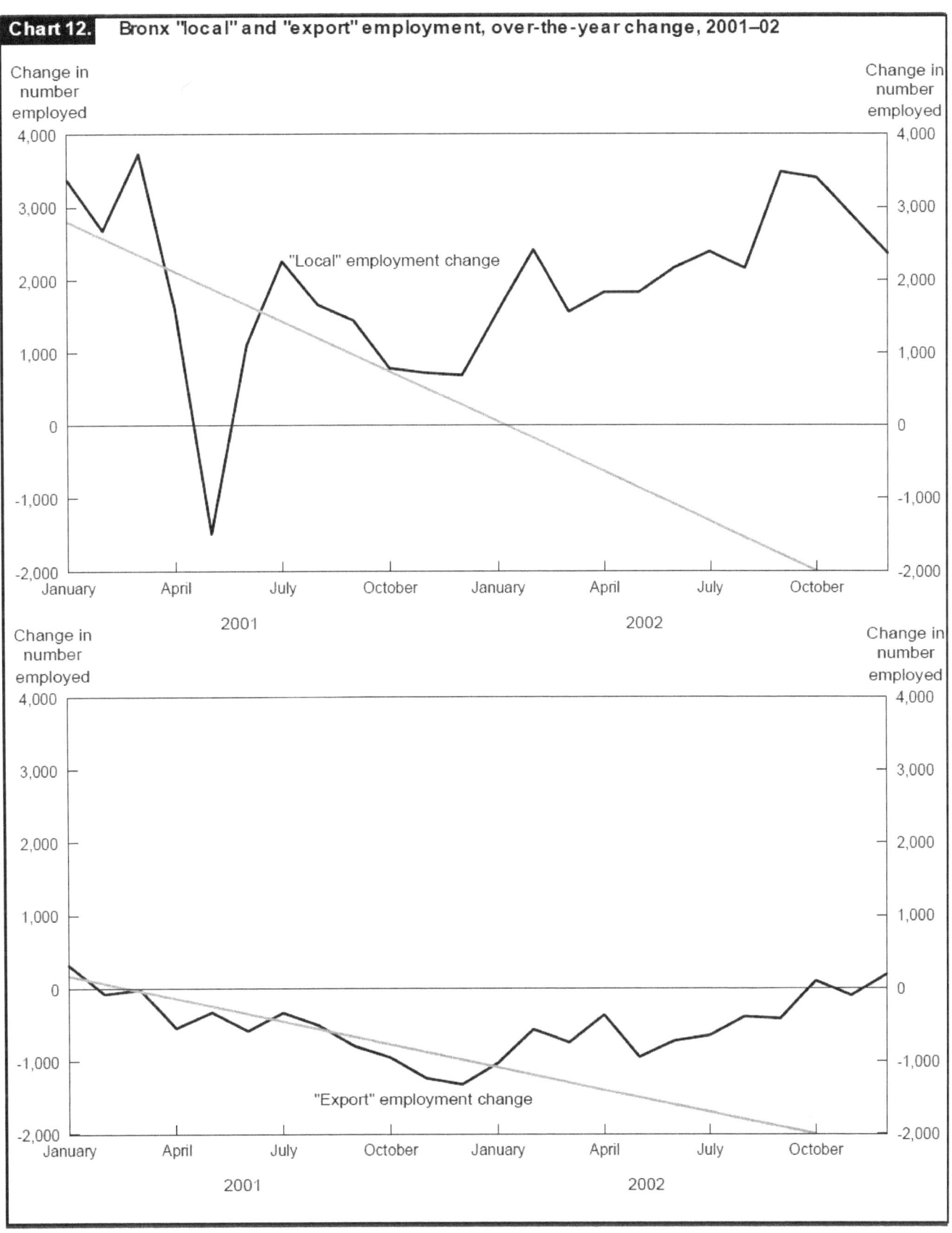

Chart 12. Bronx "local" and "export" employment, over-the-year change, 2001–02

Change in
number
employed

Change in
number
employed

"Local" employment change

4,000
3,000
2,000
1,000
0
-1,000
-2,000

January   April   July   October   January   April   July   October
2001   2002

Change in
number
employed

Change in
number
employed

"Export" employment change

4,000
3,000
2,000
1,000
0
-1,000
-2,000

January   April   July   October   January   April   July   October
2001   2002

Table 15.	Effect of 9/11 in job months and lost or gained wages over the 2000–02 period, the Bronx		
Sector	Job months	Wages, lost or gained
---	---	---
Total lost	−20,375	−$53,143,260
Finance and insurance	−50	−147,600
Professional, scientific, and technical	−450	−1,328,400
Management of companies	−250	−974,000
Real estate, and rental and leasing	−750	−1,729,950
Manufacturing	−4,675	−13,197,250
Wholesale trade	−875	−3,251,225
Retail trade	−4,400	−8,311,600
Transportation and warehousing	−675	−2,117,835
Educational services	−7,500	−20,976,900
Accommodation and food services	−375	−424,875
Other services	−375	−683,625
Total gained[1]	25,525	82,189,800
Information	625	2,470,800
Arts, entertainment, and recreation	300	1,802,100
Administrative and support, and waste	375	688,875
Construction	900	3,565,800
Health care and social assistance	23,250	73,191,000

[1] Detailed entries do not necessarily sum to totals. (See appendix.)   SOURCE: BLS QCEW program.

economy" were centered in the information sector. Two specific categories—wired telecommunications carriers and telecommunications resellers—accounted for most of the job losses in the sector.

The terrorist attack of 9/11 accounted for approximately 4,400 lost job months and about $17 million in lost wages in the Staten Island economy. (See table 18.)

Caveats and conclusions

In this article, the analysis has been limited to the employment and wages of the people who work in, and thus create, the economic life of New York City and its boroughs. The substantial economic implications of the destruction of buildings, other real estate, and the city's infrastructure, as well as the economic value of the extensive loss of life, were not a part of the analysis.

In addition, the methodology used may have underestimated the economic value of the losses in jobs and wages. Specifically, (1) if economic losses are calculated beginning in September 2001, with the trend line covering 8 months instead of 9, (2) if an economic value is placed on the jobs that were transferred to New Jersey, and (3) if the economic effect of Manhattan's finance sector is extended beyond 4 months, the losses would be substantially higher.

To place the findings in perspective, the lost wages associated with the terrorist attacks represented around 30 percent (just over $9 and a quarter billion) of the entire sum of lost wages reported in New York City between 2000 and 2002. The average wage of all jobs affected by 9/11 was $79,050, a figure higher than the average wages recorded for any individual New York City

borough. Chart 16 shows the over-the-year change in the city's employment from 2001 to 2002. The terrorist attack's effect on the city is plainly visible.

Clearly, the effect of 9/11 was centered on the city's "export economy," which represented 68.0 percent of all lost job months and 86.0 percent of all lost wages due to the attack. The average wage for lost jobs in the "export" sector was $99,930; the comparable figure for the "local" sector was $34,659. By isolating the effect of 9/11 on the city's "export economy," and taking into account the weakening national and global economies at the time, it is possible to better understand the extremely unstable economic climate that gripped the city. Throughout the past 30 years, the "export" sector has increased in prominence in New York City's economy, and it is what was damaged by the 9/11 attack.

Earlier, it was stated that there is a special quality associated with Manhattan: the borough is the core of a "global" city. Nowhere is this notion better demonstrated than in the high average wages associated with the "global-economy" jobs that dominate the Manhattan employment scene. In Manhattan, the economic power of these jobs extend beyond the city's labor market economy, influencing the economy in the borough and beyond. The Bureau of Economic Analysis has reported that, in 1969, before the city's marked shift to a "global" economy, but at one of the highest points in city employment, per capita personal income in Manhattan was 200 percent of that of the Nation as a whole.[23] By 2001, it had risen to 300 percent.

This increase in personal wealth stimulated a drive toward cultural excellence in the New York region and also supported

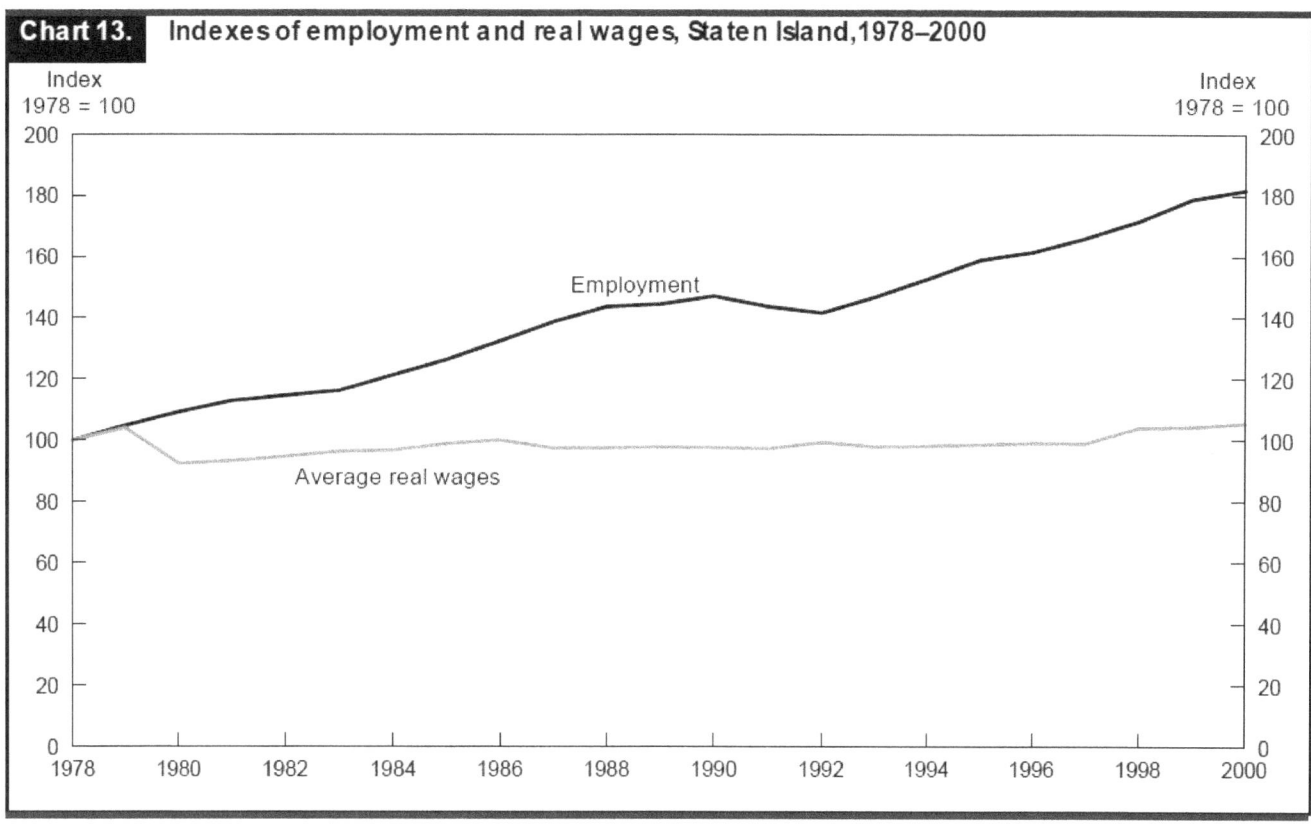

Chart 13. Indexes of employment and real wages, Staten Island,1978–2000

Index 1978 = 100

Index 1978 = 100

Employment

Average real wages

1978 1980 1982 1984 1986 1988 1990 1992 1994 1996 1998 2000

a plethora of health-care, social-services, and charitable organizations. This commitment to eleemosynary activities was underscored in 2002, when a study of the nonprofit sector reported that 14.0 percent of employees working in the city work for nonprofit organizations,

compared with 9.3 percent in the Nation.[24]

Throughout the history of the United States, New York City has played a special role in the Nation's economic development:

> What proved especially remarkable was [the city's] irrepressible ability to master the changes that so swiftly reshaped the American economy. Other cities passed from importance as their role in the national economy changed, but New York, putting to great advantage the momentum of its mighty commercial system, never relinquished its dominance.[25]

From throughout the region, the Nation, and the world, men and women have been attracted to New York by its dynamism, its opportunities, and its wealth. The "global" city has been built on the foundation of its "export economy." At issue is whether the 9/11 terrorist attack changed the city's direction. If the "export" sector was irreparably damaged, will the city ever be the same? □

Table 16. Trends in jobs, population, and wages, Staten Island, 2000 and 2002

Category	Number or amount	
	2000	2002
Total jobs	88,243	87,489
Total population	443,728	457,383
Total wages	$2,836,893,795	$2,972,024,434
Average wage	$32,149	$33,970

SOURCES: Job and wage data—BLS QCEW program; population data—U.S. Census Bureau website **http://eire.census.gov/popest/data/counties/CO-EST2003-01php** (visited April 2003).

Table 17. Employment and wages in selected sectors, Staten Island, 2000 and 2002

Sector	Average monthly employment	Percent of Staten Island employment	Total wages	Percent of total Staten Island wages	Average wage
2000					
Staten Island[1]	88,243	100.00	$2,836,893,795	100.00	$32,149
Finance and insurance	2,455	2.78	97,535,935	3.44	39,735
Professional, scientific, and technical	3,216	3.64	117,494,370	4.14	36,530
Information	3,340	3.78	172,226,026	6.07	51,565
Arts, entertainment, and recreation	1,170	1.33	24,400,681	.86	20,858
Management of companies	736	.83	31,990,084	1.13	43,494
Real estate, and rental and leasing	1,470	1.67	34,362,885	1.21	23,372
Manufacturing	1,559	1.77	57,967,054	2.04	37,172
Administrative and support, and waste	4,041	4.58	96,604,105	3.41	23,906
Construction	6,708	7.60	292,777,223	10.32	43,649
Wholesale trade	1,418	1.61	50,406,995	1.78	35,548
Retail trade	14,641	16.59	286,062,402	10.08	19,538
Transportation and warehousing	5,124	5.81	209,600,049	7.39	40,903
Educational services	4,065	4.61	143,016,311	5.04	35,185
Health care and social assistance	26,554	30.09	933,655,901	32.91	35,160
Accommodation and food services	5,417	6.14	65,771,042	2.32	12,142
Other services	3,462	3.92	64,017,989	2.26	18,490
Government	1,929	2.19	102,786,978	3.62	53,297
Unclassified	272	.31	7,528,633	.27	27,696
2002					
Staten Island[1]	87,489	100.00	2,972,024,434	100.00	33,970
Finance and insurance	2,583	2.95	106,848,963	3.60	41,364
Professional, scientific, and technical	3,386	3.87	125,948,493	4.24	37,199
Information	2,907	3.32	148,436,878	4.99	51,059
Arts, entertainment, and recreation	1,246	1.42	28,373,564	.95	22,764
Management of companies	796	.91	47,685,627	1.60	59,919
Real estate, and rental and leasing	1,442	1.65	39,735,557	1.34	27,564
Manufacturing	1,328	1.52	49,718,759	1.67	37,427
Administrative and support, and waste	3,489	3.99	76,140,341	2.56	21,826
Construction	6,357	7.27	305,008,212	10.26	47,979
Wholesale trade	1,361	1.56	52,954,804	1.78	38,911
Retail trade	14,494	16.57	305,988,352	10.30	21,111
Transportation and warehousing	4,994	5.71	221,674,664	7.46	44,385
Educational services	4,265	4.87	150,344,791	5.06	35,251
Health care and social assistance	26,717	30.54	993,753,412	33.44	37,196
Accommodation and food services	5,668	6.48	75,576,702	2.54	13,334
Other services	3,454	3.95	68,959,425	2.32	19,963
Government	1,664	1.90	110,182,638	3.71	66,235
Unclassified	702	.80	16,777,151	.56	23,902

[1] Detailed entries do not necessarily sum to totals. (See appendix.) SOURCE: BLS QCEW program.

Table 18. Effect of 9/11 in job months and lost or gained wages over the 2000–02 period, Staten Island

Sector	Job months	Wages, lost or gained
Total lost	−4,405	−$17,200,960
Professional, scientific, and technical	−540	−1,701,880
Information	−1,500	−6,609,000
Management of companies	−45	−426,195
Construction	−1,750	−7,093,100
Wholesale trade	−20	−62,260
Retail trade	−200	−342,200
Educational services	−300	−885,525
Other services	−50	−80,800
Total Gained[1]	5,060	12,374,340
Finance and insurance	450	1,483,650
Arts, entertainment, and recreation	260	479,700
Real estate, and rental and leasing	20	41,760
Administrative and support, and waste	1,800	3,628,800
Transportation and warehousing	500	1,784,500
Health care and social assistance	1,400	4,159,400
Accommodation and food services	600	616,200

[1] Detailed entries do not necessarily sum to totals. (See appendix.) SOURCE: BLS QCEW program.

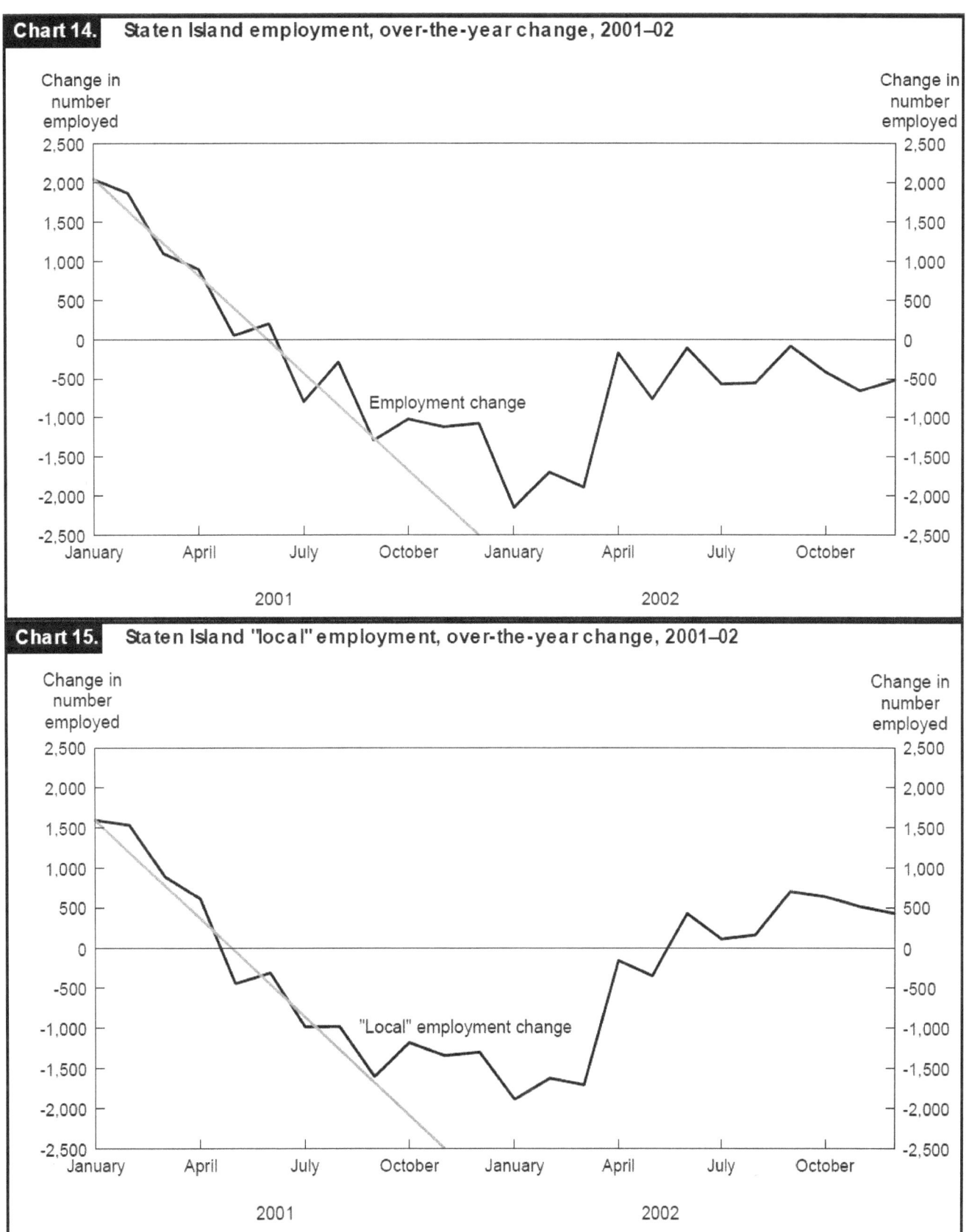

Chart 14. Staten Island employment, over-the-year change, 2001–02

Change in number employed

Employment change

January — April — July — October — January — April — July — October
2001 — 2002

Chart 15. Staten Island "local" employment, over-the-year change, 2001–02

Change in number employed

"Local" employment change

January — April — July — October — January — April — July — October
2001 — 2002

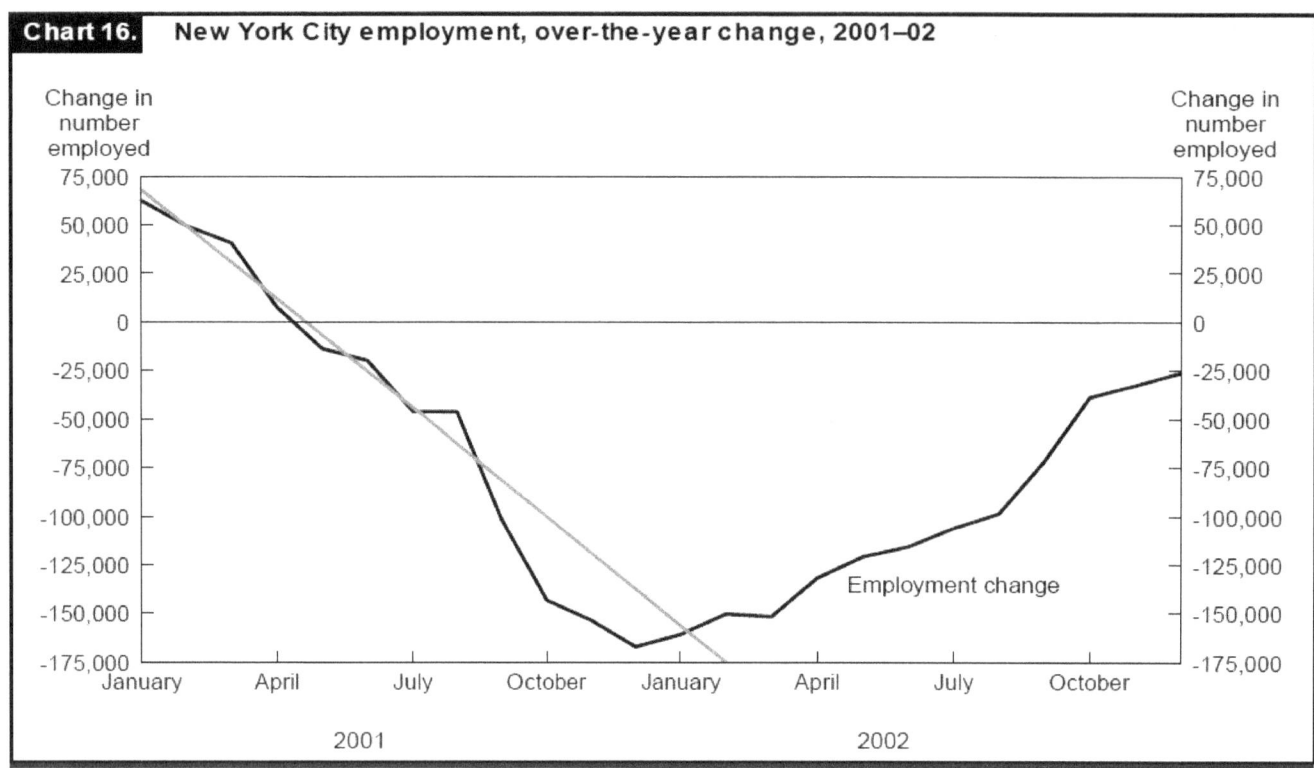

Chart 16. New York City employment, over-the-year change, 2001–02

Notes

ACKNOWLEDGMENT: The authors wish to thank the New York State Department of Labor, Division of Research and Statistics, for its role in the preparation of this article.

[1] *Work Fatalities in the New York-Northern New Jersey Area and New York City in 2001* (Bureau of Labor Statistics, New York Information Office, 2002), press release.

[2] The concept of "export" and "local" economic sectors is noted in Masahisa Fujita, Paul Krugman, and Anthony J. Venables, *The Spatial Economy Cities, Regions, and International Trade* (Cambridge, MA, MIT Press, 1999); see especially p. 27. The concept is described in Carol O' Cleireacain, "The Private Economy and the Public Budget of New York City," in Margaret E. Crahan and Alberto Vourvoulias-Bush, eds., *The City and the World New York's Global Future* (New York, Council on Foreign Relations, 1997).

[3] See Saskia Sassen, "Whose City Is It? Globalization and the Formation of New Claims," on the Internet at http://www.ifs.tu-darmstadt.de/lopofo/ak-publikationen/sassen_whose-city.pdf (visited Sept. 22, 2003); "Urban Economies and Fading Distances," on the Internet at http://www.transformaties.org/saskia_sassen.htm (visited Sept. 22, 2003); and "The Global City: Strategic Site/New Frontier," on the Internet at http://www.india-seminar.com/2001/503/503%20saskia%20sassen.htm (visited Sept. 22, 2003).

[4] *Ibid.*

[5] Over the 35 years for which there are consistent series, total Government employment in New York City has risen 11 percent, within which local government has increased by 23 percent. Federal Government employment in the city has declined during the same period. (Data from U.S. Bureau of Labor Statistics).

[6] The estimates are based on highly conservative assumptions concerning the date the effects of the attacks were first felt, the economic value of jobs transferred to New Jersey, and the duration of the impact of 9/11 in the finance sector.

[7] New York's wages were deflated by using the Consumer Price Index for the New York Consolidated Metropolitan Statistical Area. The U.S. City Average CPI was used to deflate the national figures. The charts reflect indexes of each of the series, based on 1978. The year 1978 was selected because it was the last year in which coverage was extended and, therefore, makes the series consistent to the present.

[8] Data from U.S. Census Bureau website http://www.census.gov/population/www/socdemo/journey.html (visited April 2003).

[9] Here and in what follows, all averages cited are means.

[10] The combination of increases in average wages and declines in employment must be interpreted with caution. The statistical data cited do not necessarily reflect changes in wage rates. Fluctuations in premium pay, changes in the occupational mix, or the laying off of the most recently hired workers in the preceding boom period may account for average changes in wages that do not translate into changes in the compensation of an individual worker.

[11] O' Cleireacain, "Private Economy and Public Budget," p. 27.

[12] Jason Bram, "Identification of the Beginning of the Economic Downturn in New York City," in *Current Issues*, vol. 9, no. 2, February 2003 (New York, Federal Reserve Bank of New York), pp. 2, 3.

[13] Data from BLS Current Employment Survey. Confidentiality precludes mentioning which particular jobs they were.

[14] The presupposition of a 4-month effect on the financial sector is conservative; the overall effect of 9/11 on New York City was 4 months,

and it is likely that the effect on the financial sector was longer.

[15] U.S. Census Bureau.

[16] Data from U.S. Census Bureau website **http://www.census.gov/population/www/socdemo/journey.html** (visited April 2003).

[17] The Bureau of Labor Statistics attempted to track major worker displacements linked to the terrorist actions of September 11. To develop a statistical portrait of the impact of the attacks on large-scale layoff activity, the Bureau asked employers initiating layoffs involving at least 50 workers whether their decision to call a layoff was directly or indirectly prompted by the events of that day. For the 10-week period between mid-September and mid-November, 350 mass layoffs were reported to be directly or indirectly attributable to the attacks. The actions involved 101,781 employees. New York State had 47 such layoffs involving 10,708 workers. Among the workers laid off, 42 percent, or 43,735, had been employed in the scheduled air transportation industry. An additional 29 percent, or 30,399 workers, had been employed in hotels or motels.

[18] Census data cited by Brooklyn Economic Development Corporation.

[19] The Bureau of Economic Analysis reports that there were 127,885 proprietors in Kings County (Brooklyn) and 130,823 in Queens in 2000; see "BEA Regional Accounts," on the Internet at **http://www.bea.gov/bea/regional/reis** (visited June 7, 2004).

[20] Data from U.S. Census Bureau website **http://www.census.gov/population/www/socdemo/journey.html** (visited April 2003).

[21] Data from U.S. Census Bureau website **http://www.census.gov/population/www/socdemo/journey.html** (visited April 2003).

[22] Data from U.S. Census Bureau website **http://www.census.gov/population/www/socdemo/journey.html** (visited April 2003).

[23] See "BEA Regional Accounts," on the Internet at **http://www.bea.gov/bea/regional/reis** (visited June 7, 2004).

[24] John E. Seley and Julian Wolpert, *New York City's Nonprofit Sector* (Toronto, University of Toronto Press, 2002); see especially p. 31.

[25] Thomas Kessner, *Capital City New York City and the Men behind America's Rise to Economic Dominance, 1860–1900* (New York, Simon & Shuster, 2003), p. xvi.

APPENDIX: About the data

The establishment-based data on employment and wages presented in this article come from the Covered Employment and Wages program, a cooperative program involving the Bureau of Labor Statistics of the U.S. Department of Labor and the various State Employment Security Agencies. The New York State Department of Labor Employment Security Agency provided data for this study.

Covered employment provides a virtual census (97.1 percent) of jobs on nonfarm payrolls. One source for the data is private-industry employers' quarterly tax reports on monthly employment, quarterly total and taxable wages, and contributions. Similar reports of monthly employment and quarterly wages submitted by the Federal Government and by State and local governments make up the other source.

Employees in jobs that are exempt or otherwise not covered by unemployment insurance (UI) are not included in the Covered Employment and Wages tabulations. In the private sector, these workers are wage and salary agricultural employees, self-employed farmers, self-employed nonagricultural workers, certain domestic workers, and unpaid family workers. A further group of excluded private-sector workers is covered by the railroad unemployment insurance system. In addition, a small number of State and local government workers are excluded. Certain types of nonprofit employers, such as religious organizations, are given a choice of coverage or exclusion in a number of States, so data for their employees were reported to a limited degree.

In accordance with BLS policy, data provided to the Bureau in confidence are used only for specified statistical purposes. The Bureau withholds the publication of UI-covered employment and wage data for any industry level when doing so is necessary to protect the identity of cooperating em-ployers. Totals at the industry level for the States and the Nation include the data suppressed within the detailed tables.

In keeping with the policy of nondisclosure, tables in this article do not show data separately for agriculture, mining, and utilities because of the small number of reporting units in New York in those sectors of the economy.